BE MASTER OF YOUR SELF

BE MASTER OF YOUR SELF

Robert L. Backman

Deseret Book Company
Salt Lake City, Utah

This is not an official publication of
The Church of Jesus Christ of Latter-day Saints.
The author, and he alone, is responsible
for its contents.

First printing March 1986

Library of Congress Cataloging-in-Publication Data

Backman, Robert L.
    Be master of yourself.

    Includes index.
    1. Conduct of life.   2. Success.   3. Christian life—
Mormon authors.   I. Title.
BJ1581.2.B322   1986   248.4'89332   86-2047
ISBN 0-87579-033-X

Contents

SECTION 3: OUR FAMILY SUPPORT SYSTEM

SECTION 4: HEROES AND ROLE MODELS

Section 1

LEARNING
TO MASTER
OURSELVES

1

Pushing the Limits

One man always remembered the advice he received as a child from his father. When the father would ask the boy to do chores, the boy often answered, "Do I have to? I'm too tired." To this the father would reply, "Always remember this. Most of the meaningful work in the world is done by people who are too tired to do it."

Achievement comes to those who can push beyond their limitations, whatever they may be—those who work when they don't feel like it, those who believe when everyone around them is faltering, those who hang on when hanging on seems almost too much.

It is nothing to smile when the sun is shining or to pitch in when you're filled with energy. The least among us can do that. But we find out what human beings are capable of only when they knock down old barriers and reach for something more, digging down for some power beyond the superficial sources.

Columbus was that kind of man. He tramped the roads of Europe for years. He was called a fool by all who knew him, looking for a sponsor for his grand idea. On his ships, still some days out from the New World, his men grew crazy with fear and begged him to turn back. He sailed on and changed the course of the world.

But men and women capable of pushing beyond their apparent limitations are not just figures in history books. All around us are modern adventurers of the spirit who are not afraid of the ordeal demanded by excellence. In fact, it is not fewer, but more people in this modern world who are bent on testing their mettle. Consider the marathoner. The person who ran marathons was an odd duck just a few years ago, classed somewhere between the flagpole sitter and the person who rowed the Atlantic lefthanded in winter. Not anymore. Drive down Main Street, America, and you have to dodge joggers by the dozens—all of them looking pained and winded and very virtuous.

If twenty-six miles is not enough, we have a new version of the endurance contest called the triathlon, a miserable combination of three consecutive marathons, including swimming, biking, and running a total of one hundred miles. Why would anybody withstand that kind of punishment, let alone seek it?

Larry Nielson, the first American ever to conquer Mount Everest without an oxygen tank, can give us some idea. He says there is an exhilaration in being pitted against an unforgiving taskmaster, calling forth a mental stamina that nothing else can.

On May 7, 1983, when he reached the top of the highest mountain in the world, he sat in a heap, his beard frozen with icicles, his side aching with two broken ribs, the bone showing through the skin on his ulcerated toe, coughing up blood, and famished from not having eaten for twenty-four hours. He cried, not because he hurt but because of the sheer high of his accomplishment, knowing that he was the second non-Sherpa—and the first American—to climb the 29,028-foot Everest without supplementary oxygen.

"Many people can run a marathon," Nielson said, "but if you ask them to do it a second day in a row, it narrows down the field. To do it three days in a row narrows it even more. And then it becomes a very mental problem as well as a physical one. And that's the way it is on Everest. You're wearing your body down, day after day. And it becomes a mental drive. Do you have the mental ability to continue on, or do you fold up and come home? On Everest, once you're above 18,000 feet, your body deteriorates, no matter how many calories you eat." (Ed Eaton, "Breathtaking—On Everest Without Oxygen," *This People*, September 1983.)

For Nielson, the climb was a special physical challenge. According to writer Ed Eaton, "The day before he left on his 1983 expedition, Nielson had the stitches removed from having part of a toe taken off. Suddenly, his second toe on one foot was longer and therefore acted as the big toe. The grinding pressure caused it to ulcerate, the bone showing. That happened even before advance base camp was established, and Nielson spent the rest of the expedition, which was two months, nursing and treating the toe, trying to reduce the pain. . . .

"After eating at 17,000 feet, Nielson was chosen to be in the lead party heading for the summit. When he left Camp 1, he could feel the onset of an upset stomach. By the time he spent a day on the ice and cliffs between Camps 1 and 2, he had contracted giardia, a Tibetan strain of intestinal flu, that kept him from holding down water or food."

Worst of all, however, was the struggle for oxygen, exaggerated by Nielson's dehydration. He broke two of his ribs struggling for air on the high cliffs, and he would look with envy at night at the guy next to him who had an oxygen supply to help him sleep through the night. Nielson could doze for only a few minutes before waking up in the fight for breath.

Still, despite it all, he made it to the top of the world. He scaled a mountain of ice. He fought back cold and fatigue and pain, and he'll never be the same again because of it.

As Nielson said, "For me, the conquest of Mt. Everest

was as much a spiritual one as it was physical. You just can't pit your skills against that kind of mountain if you don't have peace of mind. If anything is amiss in your life, you tend to think about it at crucial times when your concentration needs to be elsewhere. And if you make too many mistakes, Everest will beat you every time. As I stood on top of the world, I felt not only exhilaration, but a lot of gratitude for a lot of things, especially for a Father in Heaven who has stood by me on all the mountains of my life."

I think that the vigor for Larry Nielson and all the modern adventurers who work when they are too tired comes from this source. There is a great thrill in overcoming ourselves. It is far more difficult to master ourselves than to master a city—harder to discipline our weaknesses than to give in to them. It means to give up what we want this minute, for what we want in the long run. It means to delay gratification when something sweet may be right at hand.

But if Larry Nielson is to be believed, this is the only way we can become what we long to become. There is no way to move beyond ourselves without actually moving beyond ourselves. Our mountain may not be Everest. It may be something far less showy and more personal. But for every person who makes it to the top when all else has worked against him, the exhilaration will be the same.

2

Setting Our Goals
for Excellence

Life sometimes has a way of beating us down until we want to be comfortable instead of excellent, until we'd like to rest instead of run the rapids. You know how it goes. You start as a young person thinking you'd like to be brilliant at something, and then you find out how much work it would be. You discover that excellence is painful, that high standards mean hard labor. So you rethink your standards and give yourself grand excuses. "I guess I'm just an average kind of guy," you say to yourself.

That sounds all right until you remember that average is as close to the bottom as it is to the top.

How do our standards slip? This is an awesome kind of question that brings us to the realization that with every choice in life, we are not merely choosing things or events. We are choosing ourselves, for just as surely as we shape life, it shapes us. Our character is not formed in some sudden dramatic moment, but in a succession of small actions. Soon these actions become more or less automatic and we have become powerful or weak without even noticing it.

It is as Plutarch said, "Character is long-standing habit." Excellence is probably the infinite capacity for taking pains with our labor. Some even say that infinite capacity for taking pain is what genius is. If so, genius or excellence has as much to do with character as with intelligence.

No matter what materials we have to work with, we can choose to be excellent or average. In his book on excellence, John W. Gardner says that the things that have kept us from having high standards are "laziness, complacency, the desire for a fast buck, . . . shortcuts, [and] reluctance to criticize slackness." You'll notice that each of these things he has mentioned are attitudinal, not aptitudinal. This feeling is supported by a corporation president who said, "Give a young man an opportunity and he'll look for a way to avoid it." Adam S. Bennion said much the same thing: "If you want to be comfortable, take an easy job. If you aspire to leadership, take off your coat."

What these writers seem to suggest is that excellence is possible, but it doesn't just happen without intense effort. We still marvel today at the magnificent ceiling of the Sistine chapel, but it wasn't made possible by Michelangelo's genius alone. It happened because of his impeccable standards and diligence, which kept him lying on his back on a scaffold, with paint dripping in his eyes, for four pain-wracked years. Always he was driven by a compulsion to achieve. He reportedly said, "I try harder than any there ever was, ill in health and with the greatest of effort, and yet I have patience to get to the desired end."

Excellence—that infinite capacity for taking pains to achieve—also marked the work of Antonio Stradivari, widely acknowledged as the world's most superb craftsman of violins. Though his nearly seventy-five years of making violins spanned a period from 1660 to 1737, his work has never been duplicated, not with all the help of modern technology.

What was there about Stradivari's character, his mind, his heart that could transform wood and glue and varnish into an instrument that could sing? Scholars have tried to discover the secret of his excellence, but it is difficult.

Stradivari's origins are obscure. He was probably a little boy who liked to whittle violins in seventeenth-century Italy. Now, who knows how many other boys in those days liked to whittle, and maybe even some whittled violins? But young Antonio loved what he did—enough so that in his early teens he was apprenticed to Nicolo Amati, the foremost violin maker of the day. He worked as an apprentice for Amati for several years, and interestingly enough, he did not flash forth as a brilliant genius all at once. On the contrary, according to his biographers: "He was slow to develop, though from the first he showed industry, earnestness and persistency in carrying out his own ideas, whether good or bad." (William H. Hill, Arthur F. Hill, and Alfred E. Hill, *Antonio Stradivari, His Life and Work 1644-1737*, New York: Dover, 1909.) It is interesting that his earliest works do not foreshadow a man of such exceptional and versatile abilities as he later proved himself to be. But somewhere in the back of his head there must have been a shining standard for which he was aiming.

After the death of his master, when Stradivari began producing his own instruments, the greatness of the man began to slowly unfold. He seemed to have been filled with new ideas for creating violins of greater beauty and tone. He chose exquisite wood for his work, and developed deep red varnishes that had never been tried before. And always there was a sense of dedication to his purpose, unflagging effort at his workbench every day.

In fact, his biographers noted that in 1700, when he had been at his work forty years, a time when most people decline in productivity, he was just on the threshold of new and greater efforts, trying fresh ideas, each perfectly worked into an exceptional violin.

Even into his old age, well past eighty when his workman's hands must have lost some of their steadiness, Stradivari continued to produce violins. The violins he made then attest to some struggle in their making, but they still far excel almost anything else made by other craftsmen. In fact, his biographers write, "Stradivari's powers of production seemed to become more marked as his years rolled on; his energy apparently inexhaustible. . . . His sole aim in this world was his calling; and although we have but scanty knowledge concerning his daily life, we may safely assume that he was to be found day after day seated at his workbench, with gauge, compass, or knife in hand, giving form to those instruments which were to prove models of perfection for future generations."

Stradivari's sense of excellence and capacity to take pains with his work so marked his violins that experts today can readily tell if a violin was made by him without even looking at the label. He carved his spirit right into the wood. He made violins—and they made him.

On the counter of a violin shop in Salt Lake City today is a sign that says, "God be praised Antonio Stradivari had an eye that winces at false work and loved the true. And for my fame—when any master holds 'twixt chin and hand a violin of mine, he will be glad that Stradivari lived, made violins and made the best. I say not God himself can make man's best without the best men to help him. He could not make Stradivari violins without Stradivari."

3

Getting What We Want

One of the oldest debates in this world is the question of how much we personally have to say about what happens to us. Are we victims of circumstance? Are we flotsam and jetsam being tossed and washed downstream in the great current of life's activities? Do we have any control over our lives? Is there any correlation between our desires and our destinies?

Philosophers have haggled over this question for as long as philosophers have haggled (which is, I suppose, as long as there have been philosophers). It is the ancient and ever modern debate of free will versus determinism.

I don't pretend to have a detailed answer to this question, nor could I give an answer in the next couple of minutes if I had it. There are certainly sufficient examples of people who seem to be in circumstances they would not choose for themselves. This makes one leery of any broad, sweeping statements.

But having thus given a respectful acknowledgment to the pressures and circumstances that impinge on all of us, let me say what I think is a word of truth about how we do direct our own destiny. Better yet, let me quote a couple of respected thinkers on the subject of thought. Marcus Aurelius, a philosopher as well as emperor of Rome, said, "Our

11

life is what our thoughts make it." And seventeen centuries later, the New England philosopher Ralph Waldo Emerson said, "Intellect annuls fate. So far as man thinks, he is free."

How do our thoughts direct our actions and finally our lives? I remember an English play in which old Silas Marner let gold become his greatest desire. He planned his every action toward the attainment of his hoard, and he was successful. But in the process of getting his gold, he lost everything else. He achieved the useless, wasted, money-grubbing existence that such a narrow focus on money inevitably brings. Later he lost his money and mourned bitterly his ill fortune.

One morning a different kind of gold entered Silas Marner's life. It was the golden hair of a baby girl abandoned on his doorstep. He took the baby in and cared for her. Old Silas's gold-plated heart melted in the warmth of the little girl's love, and almost without his realizing it, the focus and desire of his life changed. His means and energies were only important insomuch as they gave happiness to his adopted daughter.

Silas learned an immutable truth in this world: The interest rate on the time and means we invest in others is phenomenal. It makes our capital investment of love grow faster than a blue-chip stock. His storehouse of love could not be contained. Then he found that his care and concern spilled beyond his daughter to his neighbors and others in the community. He became a new person. Where his life had been gloomy, miserable and selfish before, now it was filled with joy and satisfaction. But in one sense, there was no difference in Silas Marner before and after his change of heart. In both cases, he got what he wanted.

I believe it is safe to say that even in this imperfect and sometimes confusing world, we more often get what we want than we might choose to admit. Our desires tend to direct the way our thoughts run. We pick up subtle clues, in-

formation, and innuendos as we go through each day's activity. We stir and sift the ideas and messages that come to
us. We build networks of contacts, associations, and power
sources. We also develop within ourselves patterns of response to the opportunities and challenges that meet us
every day. This process of evolution begins to make each of
us a certain kind of person, and that, I believe, directs our
final destiny more than any other thing.

This principle works for nations as well as individuals.
The destiny of a country or a society will ultimately be directed by the desires, dreams, and aspirations of the people.
Certainly this is true in the free land of America. Americans
may be momentarily distracted and temporarily persuaded
to some fad or fashion, but ultimately it is the will and mood
of the majority that moves the nation in one direction or
another.

How, then, stands the republic? Public polls can give us
some indications, and I was encouraged by one I read recently. These are some of the results they reported.

More than anything else, Americans still cherish their
family life, according to the poll. Eighty-two percent of
those interviewed listed a good family life as their most important social value.

Good health was the next valuable possession mentioned. If we go about pursuing this goal with the proper
diet, exercise, and good health habits, this seems to me a
worthy endeavor as well.

A good self-image also rated high, as did personal satisfaction in general. Again, if we realize that both satisfaction
and a good self-image can come only from doing things we
can feel proud of, this desire should make us better people.
I'm assuming that that is what we have in mind, not some
veneer of respectability hiding behind a false front.

Americans want to live up to their potential, according
to the survey. They also want interesting work and a sense of

accomplishment. And almost two-thirds of Americans listed "following God's will" as important, while more than half listed "helping people in need."

Keeping a strict moral code and being active in church or synagogue is more important to Americans than having a nice home, car, belongings, and a high income, according to this survey. Leisure time and social recognition ranked dead last in importance.

Now, even allowing for a certain amount of polling error from people giving what seems to be a respectable answer rather than their true feelings, I still find these responses very encouraging for the future health of our nation and our people. We will fall short of our goals, of course. We will probably be shortsighted, gullible, self-seeking sometimes, and guilty of other failings. But notwithstanding this, I believe that Americans are basically good people. I believe that our history shows this and that our future destiny will reflect it. Most important, I believe that as long as such a moral code prevails in America, the God of heaven will smile down on us as he has in the past.

4

Answers to Vital Questions

Few of us today really believe that elves and goblins live among us, or that our ears burn when others speak of us, or that wounds can be cured by anointing the weapon with which they were inflicted, or that a corpse resumes bleeding in the presence of the murderer, or that amulets can ward off wrinkles, the evil eye, or the plague. Not many of us have had our family doctor prescribe leeches for bloodletting in times of sickness, or dried toads in a bag hung around the neck to try to absorb the poisonous air that brings on the plague. But it has not been so many years since these were accepted beliefs and common practices.

On the other hand, all of us enjoy comforts that would have been the envy of ancient kings and emperors. We have knowledge at our fingertips that the ancient sages would have given their lives for.

Our world was undreamed of by the people of any past age. For this knowledge and the material blessings of our times, we are indebted to the scientific method and to those who practice it.

The scientific method is probably the most productive and successful mental discipline that mankind has ever devised. It has revealed to us the mysteries of the animals and plants around us, the stars, the universe, and the physical laws by which our world functions. The chemical organization through which material things are formed, knowledge of life forms that has been the basis of modern medicine, the technology and engineering that have brought convenience and comfort to common existence—all of these and more have been achieved through the application of the scientific method in research and engineering and technology. No one can deny the debt our civilization owes to science.

But even as we praise the scientific method, it is also appropriate that we note its limitations. Science was created for very specific purposes and to answer well-defined needs. In the sixteenth century, according to historians Will and Ariel Durrant, a renewed emphasis was placed on the practical aspects of life. They write: "Men had to count and calculate, measure and design, with competitive accuracy and speed; they needed tools of observation and recording; demands arose which were met by the invention of logarithms, analytical geometry, calculus, machines, the microscope, the telescope, statistical methods, navigational guides, and astronomical instruments. Throughout Western Europe lives were henceforth dedicated to meet these needs." (*The Age of Reason Begins*, New York: Simon and Schuster, 1961, p. 163.)

Those dedicated scientists since then have fulfilled their tasks admirably, giving us far more precise information about the world we live in and ways to understand and improve it.

But there are some vital questions of this life that do not yield their answers through scientific method. These questions are the most important issues we will deal with on this earth. They include the basic question of what is life. Albert Szent Gyorgyi, a brilliant scientist and Nobel laureate, described his futile pursuit of the secret of life using the disciplines of science alone. He wrote:

"In my hunt for the secret of life, I started my research in histology. Unsatisfied by the information that cellular morphology could give me about life, I turned to physiology. Finding physiology too complex, I took up pharmacology. Still finding the situation too complicated, I turned to bacteriology. But bacteria were even too complex, so I descended to the molecular level, studying physical chemistry.

"After 20 years work, I was led to conclude that to understand life we have to descend to the electronic level, and to the world of wave mechanics. But electrons are just electrons and have no life at all. Evidently on the way I lost life; it had run out between my fingers." (Sydney Harris, "Science Loses in Search for Life," in *Deseret News*.)

This sincere scientist learned what others have learned: that the tests and measurements we use for the tangible world we are accustomed to are sometimes too crude to measure and evaluate things of the spirit.

Jesus explained some of these spiritual truths to a learned man of his day named Nicodemus. The man was a leader of his people and learned in their arts, customs, and histories, but the wisdom of Jesus baffled him. Jesus told him, "The wind bloweth where it listeth, and thou hearest the sound thereof, but canst not tell whence it cometh, and whither it goeth: so is every one that is born of the Spirit."

Nicodemus answered, "How can these things be?"

Jesus replied, "Art thou a master of Israel, and knowest not these things? . . . If I have told you earthly things, and ye believe not, how shall ye believe, if I tell you of heavenly things?" (John 3:8-10, 12.)

The secret of life slipping through our fingers, knowledge wafting past us like the wind in the trees—these are apt descriptions of attempting to gain spiritual knowledge and wisdom through earthly research methods. But this is not to say that these answers are unobtainable, or are the special province of only a chosen few. They are available to anyone who cares to seek them out and pursue them in the way the Lord has directed. And, like all truth, they can be demonstrated again and again each time the research procedures are properly followed. Jesus invited his hearers to try his doctrines and see if they came from God or if he spoke of himself.

The way to test these truths is not difficult, and it requires no special training or complicated equipment. The procedures include prayer, unselfish service, love to our fellowman, a conscious desire to know the truth, and other very valid testing procedures.

The promise of following this line of spiritual inquiry is that we will find the answers that slip through our fingers in the purely scientific method. We will get a glimpse of what life really is, its meaning, its purpose, its fulfillment.

The most important questions of our existence—who we are, where we came from, where we are going—are questions that will yield themselves to sincere inquiry through faith and prayer.

Let us search for these important answers, and when they come to us, let us follow the whisperings of the Spirit that tell us what to do. May we gain additional knowledge and build our lives on it, and so bless the lives of others.

5

Imagination—
and Something More

"There are two ways of learning how to ride a fractious horse," said Wilbur Wright in 1901. "One is to get on him and learn by actual practice how each motion and trick may be best met; the other is to sit on a fence and watch the beast a while, and then retire to the house and at leisure figure out the best way of overcoming his jumps and kicks. The latter system is the safest; but the former, on the whole, turns out the larger proportion of good riders. It is very much the same in learning to ride a flying machine: if you are looking for perfect safety, you will do well to sit on a fence and watch the birds; but if you really wish to learn, you must mount a machine and become acquainted with its tricks by actual trial."

Thus did Wilbur Wright answer his many critics who ridiculed his efforts with the flying machine. They laughed, they jibed, and they poked fun, but twenty-seven months later his brother Orville mounted their machine at Kitty Hawk, North Carolina, and flew 120 feet, and thus the air age was born.

Nearly every pioneering effort has been met with similar ridicule. An article in the initial issue of the magazine *Fly* suggested a reason. "Ninety-nine percent of the human race lack imagination," said the article. "It is this deficiency which retards progress. . . . So the individual who is capable of expanding his mind to the point where he 'sees through' [what is] not yet observed by others is usually set down as a dreamer. If he dreams above a whisper he is called a crank. There have been many dreamers and some cranks on the subject of flying machines during the past few years who have been held up to all sorts of public ridicule."

The fence-sitter, then, is not the one who moves humanity forward. It is not the security-conscious soul, the one who always has to meet with approval, who creates something new. Instead, it takes someone willing to try something different, to get off the benches and into the fray. Human progress is never made by those who are comfortable where they are.

The discomfort of our pioneering geniuses is almost legend. Dr. William Harvey discovered that blood circulates through the body—and almost got tossed out of the local medical association. His colleagues considered having him confined, and he lost many patients for his idea.

It was the same way for Rene Theophile Laennec. He was the doctor who invented the stethoscope, allowing medical men to listen into the body of their patients. "Poppycock," said his colleagues. They wouldn't use his gadget, and some even went so far as to call it the work of the devil.

Now, of course, it's easy from our vantage decades later, knowing that blood does circulate in the body and that the stethoscope does work, to marvel at those who didn't support it. But it is harder at the time to foresee the marvelous breakthroughs of the day.

Even a sage like Mark Twain missed out on a good bet. He was approached by one fellow who thought he had come up with a good gadget and wanted Twain to invest five hundred dollars in it. The humorist didn't think there was much future in it—and he therefore lost his chance to become a part of Alexander Graham Bell's new communication device, the telephone.

What all of this resistance to innovation tells us is that the mob isn't really as smart as we think it is. To use a reference point that "everybody says so" has its dangers. "Everybody" doesn't know that much. Too often those who have a slightly different view are seen as half-cocked. Dreamers are dismissed. But think about it: where would we be without them? Every step forward has been made because somebody had an idea that shook the status quo.

Surprisingly, it has been the experts who have been fooled most often, maybe because they were so sure of their answers that they didn't admit deviation. How many of those who have gone on to change the world have been labeled incompetent by those who were supposed to be in the know? Enrico Caruso, whose rich voice thrilled millions, was told by a singing teacher in his early years to get out of the business because he didn't have a voice. A Kansas City newspaper editor looked at some drawings of an aspiring artist and told him he couldn't draw cartoons. Luckily Walt Disney didn't believe him. It's amazing how often the big brains of the day have been wrong.

Those who have pushed humanity forward, then, have been those who have had imagination—and something more. They have had the courage to stick by their idea even when the crowd laughed or the experts booed. Perhaps humanity would move even faster if more of us were to develop those characteristics. How many ideas have been discarded before they had chance to take root because their owners were fearful? How many have quit because the experts said they were not worthy?

As Dan Valentine said, "It has always been unpopular

to break trails in the path of progress." And it probably always will be. But we can be thankful that a few souls trust themselves and their ideas enough to start out on unmarked trails. We can be grateful for those who have the vision to see what can be developed from small beginnings.

6

Some Secrets of Success

Researchers at the Peak Performance Center in California have studied the most productive people in athletics, business, education, the arts, and other fields to see if there are common threads among these effective performers. There are some similarities, they have found.

One mild surprise is that peak performers generally live well-rounded lives. This may contradict the image we have had of the narrow-minded specialist who spends his whole life perfecting his skills in one area. The dumb athlete, the bespectacled egghead, the ulcer-afflicted high-pressure businessman—these apparently are stereotypes we have created. In reality, the top performers seem to lead well-balanced, diversified lives. They know how to relax and how to enjoy the beauty and aesthetics of life. They have friends and are apparently a lot like people everywhere.

A second finding from the researchers is that we do better if we choose a career we care about. I think this is particularly relevant in today's world of work. Things are changing so rapidly that to just focus on a career because that seems to be where the big money is today may leave one vulnerable to social and technological changes that may make that career obsolete.

And even if it doesn't, suppose a person were successful

and made piles of money. Would it be sufficient to pay him for spending a major part of his adult life in a vocational prison of his own making? I have a friend who has a beautiful baritone voice. He was a practicing lawyer when he finally decided that his music meant more to him than any amount of money. Today, midway through a career that has touched the lives of thousands of students and thrilled those of us who have shared his gift, he is a happy man. He, his wife, and his family have never regretted his decision.

So find out what you love to do and do it. You will probably be more successful.

Another common misconception is that top performers are perfectionists. Obviously, they don't do sloppy, slipshod work. They do excellent work. But they don't do perfect work. And they are not afraid to reach out and try something that may be a bit beyond their grasp even if it leaves them open to criticism, and even if they fail. Generally speaking, a significant body of good work will do more for the world and for an individual than waiting for that great and perfect masterpiece to emerge.

Peak performers are not afraid to take risks. Most of us are tempted to hide in our comfort zones doing the things we feel sure about. But it is probably true that we learn more from our mistakes than we do from our successes.

One of the most famous examples of weathering failure is Thomas Edison's legendary pursuit of a filament for his electric light bulb. He tried virtually everything he could get his hands on. His first success came from raiding Mrs. Edison's sewing basket for thread. That worked, but not well enough. And so he tried unsuccessfully all the known metals that might glow inside a vacuum glass bulb. Then he began making his way through the animal and vegetable kingdoms. He tried bones, hooves, hides, horns, apple peels, lemon rinds, onions, string beans, macaroni, grass, rope plants, every conceivable kind of wood, and literally hundreds of other substances. He finally resorted to peeling off long strips of anything that fell under his glance. Visitors to his laboratory learned to keep their umbrellas and canes with them, because if they left them behind the door, a long strip might be sliced off as a contribution to electric light research.

Hundreds of times those filaments burned out. But one day Edison looked up from his work and saw a bamboo fan lying nearby that his assistants had been using to cool a chemical. Of course, he picked it up, peeled off a sliver, mounted it in his glass bulb, and *voila!*—there was light.

Someone once asked Edison if he felt all those experimental failures were a waste of time and money. "Certainly not," he replied. "They showed us all the things that wouldn't work."

Thus, we can all learn to take a few risks, stretch ourselves, and stay out of the comfort zone as much as we can. We all like to feel secure in what we do, but the road to security may also be the trail to stagnation.

There is one world in which we can focus on success and reap rich benefits. This is the world inside our own head. It is vital that we picture ourselves succeeding, according to the experts. Championship athletes spend a lot of time doing this. A pianist in China, imprisoned for seven years during the Cultural Revolution, played as well as ever soon after he was released, though he hadn't touched a piano in all those years. He said, "I practiced every day in my mind."

The theater of the mind can be a powerful motivator. And since we own the theater, we might as well write our own scripts, star in our own shows, and create our own happy endings. We may be surprised at how often those same scenarios get played out in our real life.

The final word of advice from the experts is that we shouldn't underestimate our abilities. I have read a number of estimates on the potential of the human brain, and I have yet to read one that claims we use more than ten to fifteen percent of our potential. We all have vast untapped powers waiting to be utilized.

Many years ago I read a comparison of the human brain with a computer. The article said that to equal the capacity of a child's brain would require a computer the size of the mammoth Pentagon Building in Washington. I used that comparison for several years, but then a friend who is a computer expert corrected me and said, "That's no longer accurate. We have developed such small and sophisticated computers today that we can just about duplicate the human brain's storage capacity in a computer of the same size."

So I stopped using that impressive analogy. Then, just a few weeks ago, I read another one. Using these sophisticated computers, we have found out even more about the human brain, and specifically how well it can not only hold information but also mulch and mix it and create with it. To simulate those functions of that three pounds of gray matter that we carry around would require a computer ten stories high that would cover the state of Texas. That's right—our brain is a Texas-size thinking, feeling, and creating machine that far outstrips anything in our universe. And there is more yet to discover about who and what we are as human beings.

The most important point in this evaluation and motivation exercise is that each of us has the power, the right, and, yes, the responsibility to succeed. This doesn't mean we have to rule the world or be the idol of millions. The ultimate success is to become all that we have the potential to be. And the deepest sadness of this life or the next would be to look back and see chances and opportunities we didn't take, to learn that we cut ourselves short and let others down when we could have helped them, to realize that we could have helped more if we had developed our talents and used them to serve others.

Somebody once said, "It's okay to be mediocre as long as you're the best at it." Our little efforts might look mediocre to some people, but if they are our best, they will feel good to us.

7

Four Steps
to Self-Renewal

The beginning of each new year is when most of us sit down to make our resolutions. We'd like to make changes. We think we'd be happier if we did. But too often even our best ideas seem like no more than giving a new paint job to a used car. We know it will still rattle and its heart will be the same.

What we really need during dark winter days is the secret to self-renewal. How is it that some people have the regenerative power to continually face life with new vigor, flexibility, and creativity, while so many merely stagnate? Why are some receptive, curious, eager, unafraid, and willing to try anything, while the rest of us go to seed?

Self-renewal is a rare ability, but writer John W. Gardner gives four steps to achieving it.

The first step is that we continue to learn as long as we live. That sounds easy enough. The opportunities for doing so are all around. Yet, the truth is that most of us are absolutely mummified by middle age. Self-development is blocked by the individual's own intricately designed, self-imposed barriers. As Gardner says, "Many young people have stopped learning in the religious or spiritual dimensions of their lives long before they graduate from college. Some settle into rigid and unchanging political and economic views by the time they are twenty-five or thirty. By their mid-thirties, most will have stopped acquiring new skills or new attitudes in any central aspect of their lives.

"As we mature we progressively narrow the scope and variety of our lives. Of all the interests we might pursue, we settle on a few. Of all the people with whom we might associate, we select a small number. We become caught in a web of fixed relationships. We develop set ways of doing things." (*Self-Renewal: The Individual and the Innovative Society*, New York: Norton, 1983, p. 9.)

We lose the ability to see the world with fresh perceptions; our eyes are dim as we look at the features of our everyday world. That is why travel becomes such a vivid experience for us. At home we have lost the ability to see what is right before us, and travel refreshes our perspective.

It is interesting too that we all have talents and abilities that remain untapped throughout our lifetime. Gardner compares us to gold mines that were worked for a little while and then abandoned before the richest veins were found. The circumstances of our lives teach us to call forth certain talents, but that doesn't mean they are the only talents we have. The self-renewing person will thrust himself into circumstances that call forth new abilities. He will seek to work the full range of personal possibilities, rather than let them be limited by habit or routine.

Gardner's second step for self-renewal is that those who bring freshness and eagerness to life are those who have developed the courage to fail. Older people are generally less willing to take risks than are younger ones, and, consequently, their opportunities to learn and grow are narrowed.

Watch an infant sometime, and you can see this principle at work. Failure has little power to discourage a baby.

When he wants to learn something, he just tries again and again until it is accomplished, undevastated by his blunders along the way. That is one reason why babies learn at such a phenomenal rate. But as we grow older, we become less blithe about failure, until by middle age we have a long list of things we will never try because we think we might not do well at them. We hold success to be too precious, and self-esteem demands a certain level of performance.

But we pay a heavy price for our fear of failure. It is a confinement of the most smothering sort. It appears safe, but it is anything but safe. Fearing to fail, we limit what we try and become bored and boring.

To be a self-renewing person, we must recognize an essential fact about learning. It is extremely risky business. No one can explore, experiment, and progress without falling on his face a fair number of times. When Max Planck was awarded the Nobel Prize, he said, "Looking back . . . over the long . . . path which finally [led to the discovery of the quantum theory], I am vividly reminded of Goethe's saying that men will always be making mistakes as long as they are striving after something." (As quoted in Gardner, *op. cit..*)

The day we are too frightened to make mistakes is the day we are caught in a hopeless rut.

The third step to self-renewal is in self-knowledge. It is a habit with many of us, as we progress through life, to fill our days and minds with so many diversions, worries, and concerns, to so thoroughly stuff our skulls with knowledge, that we have little time to become acquainted with ourselves. In fact, one of the reasons we stuff our lives so full is to avoid the sometimes fearful job of objectively evaluating ourselves and accepting who we are. Yet the fact is that the more we come to know and depend on our own resources, the happier we are. The self-renewing person finds sustenance in the spring of his own being and is not afraid to be alone. There is new life to be found in our solitary times.

The fourth step to self-renewal is motivation. As Gardner said, "The walls that hem a man in as he grows older form channels of least resistance. If he stays in the channels, all is easy. To get out requires some extra drive, enthusiasm or energy."

Motivation comes in part from sheer physical energy and good health. To approach life with vigor takes the vitality and resistance of a healthy body. The person who is interested in self-renewal will take the greatest concern over the function and well-being of his physical body.

Beyond that, most of us have noted the astonishing sources of energy available to those who enjoy or find meaning in what they are doing. Yet often, as Gardner says, "The conventions and artificialities of life, to say nothing of habit, routine and simple momentum, carry us so far from the sources of our interest and conviction that we all need a few primer lessons in how to get back in tune with our own being."

It is essential that we cut through the false fronts of our lives to touch and feel the things that really matter to us. We can do so by following these four steps to self-renewal: continuing to learn, having the courage to fail, developing self-knowledge, and becoming motivated.

8

Mountains of Success

We often speak of climbing the ladder of success, but as newspaper columnist Sydney Harris notes, that is not a very accurate metaphor. Success is not a ladder. It is more like a mountain.

Mr. Harris writes: "A ladder proceeds vertically, rung by rung, with each rung evenly spaced, and with the whole apparatus leaning against a relatively flat and even surface. A child can climb a ladder as easily as an adult, and perhaps with a surer footing.

"Making the ascent in one's vocation or profession is far less like ladder-climbing than mountain-climbing. . . . Going up a mountain requires a variety of skills, and includes a diversity of dangers that are in no way involved in mounting a ladder.

"Young people starting out should be told this, both to dampen their expectations and to allay their disappointments. A mountain is rough and precipitous, with uncertain footing, a predictable number of falls and scrapes, and sometimes one has to take the long way around to reach the shortest distance.

"One needs different tools, and the knowledge and skill to use them most effectively. . . . Most of all, a peculiar combination of daring and prudence is called for, which not all persons possess.

"The art of 'rappeling' is important, because sometimes one has to go down a little in order to go up. And the higher one gets, the greater the risk and the greater the fall." ("Way to Success Is Not a Ladder," in *Deseret News.*)

Yes, climbing a mountain is a lot like the real world we struggle to succeed in. There is often no clearly marked-out path. There are often hidden dangers. The trail that worked for one may not work for another. It may have washed out since it was last used. Many trails to the top can only be used once. Anyone who follows the footsteps of a pioneering trailblazer may find that he becomes only a mediocre copy of the original success story.

And just as weather may wash out a mountain trail, so the demands for success in a given field may change. This requires that the success seeker or mountain climber be constantly looking for new ways to ascend the peaks. Achieving success, like climbing mountains, can be exhilarating but risky business.

So why do we struggle so hard to succeed? Someone has suggested that any person who wants to be president of the United States should be automatically ruled out on the basis of mental instability. Anybody who would wish that on himself can't be very bright, according to this line of thinking. Well, that's somewhat cynical, and excludes the desire to serve that true statesmen possess, but the point is well taken. Success usually takes a total commitment and often exacts a heavy toll, whether the contest is in politics, sports, business, or any other field of human endeavor.

Moreover, those who have ascended the heights assure us that the seat of success is not a comfortable throne so much as it is the top of a greasy flagpole, and it is easier to get up there than to stay up there.

One of my favorite football teams has been winning fairly consistently for a number of years. I have also noticed that their opponents usually play some of their finest football against this team. They gear up all year to knock over the champions. And, of course, that is the price you pay for being a champion.

What does it take to climb the mountains of success in one's occupation? Frankly, we don't know for sure. A friend of mine is a university professor who teaches business. For years he has seen bright young people pass through his program, their eyes agleam, their expectations high for what they will achieve in the world of business. He has tracked their progress and has come to some private conclusions. The students have had all different types and styles of personality, work habits, and dispositions. Some have shown more promise than others, naturally, but my friend says that often the brightest and most motivated have not done as well in their careers as others who seemed less endowed. He says that from his observations, one factor overrides all others in determining success in business. That factor is luck, pure and simple. That observation won't sell many books on business success, but that is his conclusion.

If success is so hazardous, iffy, tentative, and temporary, why do we continue to pursue it? For one thing, it is the nature of human beings to want to improve themselves and their station in life. To return to the mountain metaphor, remember Sir Edmund Hillary. He was the first to conquer this earth's highest peak, Mount Everest in the Himalayas. When he was asked why he did such a dangerous and audacious thing, he replied, "Because it's there."

The mountains of success are there too, and that is reason enough for some people to try to scale them. There is nothing wrong with wanting to succeed in one's vocation, but if worldly success were all we had to hope for in this life, perhaps few of us would try to succeed. Fewer still would actually see the summits from a distance, and only an infinitesimal fraction of the human race would ever attain the top pinnacles. The rest of us would be strewn along the trail below.

Fortunately, true success in life does not depend on outward awards and accomplishments. Real success is inside us. The way to this success is not easy either, but it is within the reach of every person. Jesus spoke of this ascending trail when he said, "Strait is the gate, and narrow is the way, that leadeth unto life." (Matthew 7:14.)

The road to personal success can be long, arduous, and frustrating. Sometimes it may require changes and detours, but on this road the destination is sure, and the grade is adapted to our individual strength. It will challenge the strongest of us, but it will also be within reach of the weakest. Our success will not be judged by the whims of the fickle world about us. Our Father in heaven will reward us on eternal principles, and the success we achieve will be exactly what we have merited.

The criteria for success will not be the wealth, power, or fame we have accumulated in this world. We will be judged according to the character we have developed and how well we have served our fellowmen.

9

Formulas for Happiness

The poet Walt Whitman wrote these lines in "Facing Westward from California's Shores" just as America's westward thrust was winding down: "Where is what I started for so long ago? / And why is it yet unfound?"

These are questions that echo meaningfully for us in a time when Americans are still rushing to find something. The frontier is the last century's dream, but we have our own images of success and happiness just over the hill. Most of us spend our lives knowing we want something, and want it badly. Some call it fulfillment, some call it peace; but whatever we name it, we chase it hard and often find it elusive. In fact, an article in *U. S. News and World Report* said, "In an era of rising affluence and leisure time, Americans are finding happiness more elusive than ever before." ("Pursuit of Happiness—Elusive Goal in America," August 27, 1973.)

Americans began this century by chanting such slogans as "Every day in every way, I'm getting better and better." Their children read such books as *The Power of Positive Thinking*, and now their grandchildren read *I'm OK, You're OK*. The material differs but the meaning is the same. We're all pleading for somebody to teach us how to be happy.

We look for happiness in the consumer market, and

36

manufacturers want to please us. They package everything
from aspirins to deodorants to cheap transmission jobs as
the answer to happiness. We seek happiness in leisure time,
hoping that watching television or skiing or backpacking
into the mountains will do the job. Even employers are on to
this basic human yearning for happiness. Many companies
try to generate employee enthusiasm for a new project by
calling it "fun."

But I'm convinced that this yearning for happiness
often remains unfulfilled because we look for it outside ourselves in things or events that can never grant it. Instead,
happiness is an inner event. It is an overcoming of that isola-
tion and alienation so many feel that makes them unable to
care passionately about their pleasures or disasters, much
less the community and world about them. It is assuming
responsibility for our own lives and choices rather than
forever feeling victimized by circumstances too big for us. In
a world that markets formulas for happiness on every best-
seller list, there is one formula for happiness that always
works. It was evident in the life of Jesus Christ. Here are five
happiness principles from his life:

1. Jesus Christ believed in something. He knew the
truth, and it made him free. When our personal commit-
ments to a value system are limited, we are made miserable.
We become wanderers in a desert without landmarks. If our
belief is not firmly rested somewhere, we are restless. Values
that change with the situation are not vital enough for us to
build a life on. There may be those who say that Christ had
an advantage in knowing the truth and being committed to
it. But he wants us to have the same advantage, and he has
given us scripture and prayer as helps to finding that solid
foundation.

2. Jesus Christ knew who he was. People taunted him
at his crucifixion, saying that if he were really the Son of
God, he could come down from the cross and end his mis-

FORMULAS FOR HAPPINESS

ery. He had no need to prove himself. His sense of self was firmly rooted inside without the need for validation that we so constantly seek. Often our identities are fragile. We easily fall into the temptation to dislike ourselves and call ourselves worthless. That is because we fail to see ourselves as God sees us. To him, we are so important that our eternal-life goal is his goal. The very Creator of the universe says that he will take time to answer our prayers. That should tell us something about how important we are in his eyes.

3. Jesus Christ was willing to sacrifice for important goals. He did not succumb to the pleasures or temptations of the moment, but always kept the greater good in mind. Those who cannot sacrifice are those who lose the vision of what is important and where they are going. Jesus always knew where he was going. His great goal was to atone for our sins and provide a way so that we might be resurrected one day, and no pain or trial could move him from that. No one can be happy who does not hold something important enough to be willing to sacrifice for it.

4. Jesus Christ sought help through prayer. Too many of us try to make life a do-it-yourself project and then are surprised when we run up against our limitations. Yet for each of us, life is like picking our way through an unmarked forest. Paths are not always clear, nor are solutions easy. But if we will rely on the Lord, he can give us directions, solutions that we might not ever come to alone. When the Savior chose his apostles, he prayed all night for preparation and guidance. When he began his mission, he went into the mountains to fast forty days and forty nights to draw close to his Father. We must do the same in our own lives.

5. Jesus Christ served others. A life can never be happy that is focused inward. If you are miserable now, march right out your door and find someone who needs you. Where in the Savior's life do we ever see an expression of concern for his own well-being? And yet his inner contentment and

peace amazed all who saw him. Loving someone else deeply is one of the most joyous feelings we can ever know. Just think how much that joy can grow if we expand our love and service to more and more people.

Happiness does not need to be elusive. Dr. George Kateb, professor of political science at Amherst, said, "The problem is to find pleasures worthy of humanity, within the reach of all, not liable to cloy and weary when experienced continuously." Jesus Christ has already shown us how to obtain those pleasures.

10

Placing Our Trust in the Lord

He'd said to trust him,
To just keep following and trust him.
We wandered on and on.
Sometimes we were in beautiful meadows
*   of clover,*
Or lush green forests
Or dazzling canyons,
But other times we traveled through
*   infested swamps*
Or scorching deserts.

These times were almost unbearable,
And I often had to remind myself
I must keep following.
But then we reached a towering mountain,
So tall I could barely see the top.
He started straight up the steep pathway
With me following,
One step, then another;
How could I take any more?

"Can't we stop?" I screamed.
Oh, how I wanted to just quit,

To fall to the earth
And let myself roll back down the
mountain!
He said nothing, but just continued on
With me somehow following.
Up and up and up and up we climbed,
Finally reaching the top.

I stumbled more than walked down the
other side of the mountain,
But reaching the bottom
I saw we were in the most beautiful place
one could behold.
I wanted to stay there forever.
He smiled at me and spoke:
"You may rest now," he said softly as I
dropped to my knees.
"You may rest in this peaceful place for
eternity."

My soul was filled with more content
Than I ever thought possible.
He had said, "Trust me."
He had brought me through trials,
And he had finally led me home.

That is as wise a piece of literature as I have ever read. If a man or a nation or this world spent a lifetime and drew out that one message from the experiences in this vale of tears, it would be a work well done.

To know that our hope and our happiness in this world depend on how we trust in the Lord; to know that the way will not be easy, but that he will walk beside us and before us; to know that he will lead us, support us, and sustain us; and to know that partially in this life, and fully in the life to come, we can find the peaceful pastures that lie beyond the rugged mountains of our lives: This is wisdom.

Many millions have lived and died on this earth and never found these holy truths. Many wise and learned persons have let these truths elude them. So it may come as a surprise that these beautiful words and profound insights come from the pen of a teenage girl, my cousin, Karen Backman. Whenever I hear people talk about today's youth as being shallow, scatter-brained, and prone to sin, I think about this poem from Karen, and I say to myself, "Some young people are that way, but not all."

How did she obtain such depth and wisdom? By paying a great price. Life is not easy for her. She has a disease that has taken most of her sight, her hearing, and her voice. Is she handicapped then? That depends on your definition.

Is Karen handicapped because she cannot hear many of the words of this world, or are we more handicapped because we have let the voices of the world drown out the whisperings of the Lord's Spirit to our inward souls?

Is Karen handicapped because she can only dimly see the light that reflects objects of this world to her eyes, or are we the handicapped ones who would let what Jesus called a "beam" in our eyes keep us from seeing our own faults instead of staring at the faults of others? How good is our vision when we focus our eyes and hearts on the things of this world and ignore far more precious gifts of the spirit?

Is Karen handicapped because her voice is soft, sometimes inaudible, or are they more handicapped who would use their lungs and tongues and voices to speak worthless prattle, gossip, or lies? I wish that all the world would whisper the name of God with the reverence she does and cease from swearing and obscenities. "Be still, and know that I am God." So spoke the Lord to the ancient Psalmist of the Bible. (Psalm 46:10.) Karen has learned this lesson well.

The point of this is not who is or is not handicapped in this world, but rather that there are certain lessons we must learn if we are to live successfully. One of these lessons is to trust in the Lord.

Suppose we were stranded on a dangerous street in the dark of night with only a vague sense of how to grope our way to safety. If someone offered us a strong sure hand to lead us out of danger, would we not grasp that hand with both of ours, hang on tightly, follow faithfully, and bless the one who had brought us safely through the danger?

Yet here we stand, an entire world on the brink of destruction. War, hatred, and killing go on all around us. Only the pressing of a few critical buttons stands between us and nuclear holocaust. Crime, deadly drugs, and destructive habits are destroying the inner fiber of our country and all that we hold dear. But when the Lord holds out his hand and offers us his light to guide us back from the precipice, how slow and reluctant we are to follow. How tenaciously we cling to sinful habits and practices. How we love to dangle one foot over the edge of the cliff and tempt the winds of fate to blow us over.

Old King Solomon was a man of some considerable experience in statecraft. He was not always successful, and he didn't always follow the wisdom he has been credited with. But he did leave us this pearl among others from his experience. He said, "Trust in the Lord with all thine heart; and lean not unto thine own understanding." (Proverbs 3:5.)

This is not to belittle the place of knowledge in our lives. Heaven knows we need all the knowledge we can lay our hands and our brains on in this complicated world. But it is to recognize the limits of rational learning. Ralph Waldo Emerson said, "Wisdom has its root in goodness, and not goodness its root in wisdom." I believe that this is true. I believe that we cannot find our way to salvation either in this life or in the world to come through the use of our intellect alone.

To be truly wise, we must be good, and goodness comes as we put our trust in the Lord and follow his counsel to us. Only this kind of wisdom can bring us out of the morass we have gotten ourselves into.

11

The Memorials of Men

I met a traveler from an antique land
Who said: Two vast and trunkless legs of stone
Stand in the desert. . . .
And on the pedestal these words appear:
"My name is Ozymandias, king of kings:
Look on my works, ye Mighty, and despair!"
Nothing beside remains. Round the decay
Of that colossal wreck, boundless and bare
The lone and level sands stretch far away.

So writes Percy Bysshe Shelley of the efforts mankind makes to memorialize itself. Our history is dotted with strange and sometimes sad attempts to memorialize and immortalize our lives.

The pyramids in Egypt and South America, the statues dotted across the world, the cities named after notable people, the empires and kingdoms set up in the name of a Caesar or a czar—these are at best quaint historical reminders of man's feeble efforts to be remembered. But, as we know, the hardest granite eventually weathers back to the ground. The steel statue will rust, corrode, and oxydize into the air. The mighty kingdom and empires built by men often do not outlive their founders very long. The great names pass and are forgotten.

45

What, then, is the real memorial to a person's life? Obviously, it is the life itself. A life lived well does not require pyramids, palaces, pomp, or power to make it significant. It stands on its own merits as a contribution to the history of the world and a proud memorial to the one who lived it. A person living such a life does not need to prove his worth or hedge up his fears against death by elaborate material things. Such a person does not even have to live long, just well.

Some time ago a young man named David Silvester, who was facing what might have been a tragic premature death, wrote this letter:

"I am not a . . . philosopher—I am a student and my learning shows me new things every day—and God shows me new things every day. I am happy—I pray I will be happy with death.

"I enjoy everything about life (almost—sickness and pain aren't too cool) and I still yearn with every particle to be able to marry and have children, and there's so much left to do that I haven't done. . . .

"Change. [Death] is just another change. Change always gets me nervous and apprehensive and antsy. But I'm always excited by it. Do I have enough time to get my life in order? . . . Maybe I'm . . . an alarmist, but I think the tumor's back . . . and if it is back then it's growing quite rapidly and I probably won't have many months left. One last chance to prove I'm worthy of eternal life with my Heavenly Father. I cried a little (two tears) about it last night.

"It is easy to believe in life after death and salvation and exaltation—but to come face to face with it is bewildering. You know . . . that there will be resurrection and assumption of rewards, but what really goes on in paradise? How will I receive the pleasure I now do from writing and reading and associating with family and friends? I . . . believe that it will continue there, but I'm still frustrated because I don't want to miss out on everything that is going on here—but then right now I am missing out on what's going on there." (Neal A. Maxwell, *We Will Prove Them Herewith*, Deseret Book, 1982, p. 33.)

What a marvelous young man! A tumor took away his life but not his faith. What wisdom, what insight, what depth of faith! Surely this young man has learned the main lesson of this life, and that is to live it well, go forward in faith, and not fear death.

William Cullen Bryant put it this way in the last part of his poem "Thanatopsis":

> *So live that when thy summons comes to join*
> *The innumerable caravan that moves*
> *To that mysterious realm, where each shall take*
> *His chamber in the silent halls of death,*
> *Thou go not, like the quarry-slave at night,*
> *Scourged to his dungeon, but, sustained and soothed*
> *By an unfaltering trust, approach thy grave*
> *Like one who wraps the drapery of his couch*
> *About him, and lies down to pleasant dreams.*

We can be sustained and soothed in the face of death either imminent or eventual. We need only follow in the footsteps of Him who conquered death. Remember again Jesus' words to the weeping Martha as she grieved over her dead brother, Lazarus. He said to her, "I am the resurrection, and the life: he that believeth in me, though he were dead, yet shall he live: and whosoever liveth and believeth in me shall never die." (John 11:25-26.)

Let us remember those good people who have gone before us. Let us praise their deeds and their lives. More importantly, let us give them the greatest tribute of all by living our own lives in such a way that we shall be worthy of honest appreciation for our labors here. Let us be a service to our fellowmen so that we may thereby quietly and confidently look to the day when we shall make the transition from this world into the next one.

And as for erecting any monuments to our memory, perhaps the counsel of the Roman statesman Pliny the Younger is as good as we could find. He lived in the days when statues, buildings, and sculptured paraphernalia proliferated as Roman generals and statesmen struggled to immortalize their names and deeds. But Pliny took a dim view of their efforts. He wrote, "The erection of a monument is superfluous; our memory will endure if our lives have deserved it."

12

Death Shall Be No More

I love the following story by Judy Kitterman and Harry Pritchett:

"Phillip was a little boy in a class of eight-year-olds in Sunday School. He was born with Down's Syndrome. He was happy, but as he grew, he became aware of ways in which he was different from other children his age. The teacher tried hard to have the ten boys and girls be a group, but it did not always work.

"The teacher had a plan for the Sunday after Easter. He collected the big eggs that panty hose come in and asked the children to go outside and find a symbol for new life, put it in the egg as if it were a secret, and come back. The children did, and put the eggs on the table in their classroom, after which the teacher opened them up, one by one. There was a flower, a butterfly, and a rock, and usually it was accompanied by 'ooh' and 'aah.'

"Then the teacher opened the next egg—and it was empty. The children cried out 'not fair' and 'stupid.' And then the teacher felt a tug on his sleeve—it was Phillip. 'That's mine,' he said. 'It's empty—the tomb was empty.' The class was silent. Then a miracle happened. That day Phillip entered the group. He was out of the tomb called 'different.'

"Phillip died last summer. His body could not fight off infection as other bodies can. His family knew his life would be short. And on the day of that funeral, nine eight-year-olds marched right up to the altar—not with flowers to cover up the stark reality of death, but with an empty egg, an empty, discarded egg.

"Perhaps that says something to us about our Easter and how we will celebrate it." (*Prayer Fellowship of Christian Scouters Newsletter*, April 1983, p. 1.)

The real essence of Easter, it seems to me, is not the absence of death but the presence of life. There may be a multitude of empty tombs, caves, and crypts in this world, but there is one sacred spot in which the true nature of our universe was displayed on that first Easter morning. Light and life overcame darkness and death in that quiet tomb.

Unfortunately, much of the world seems to have lost faith in that fact. Today the general feeling seems to be that life is a temporary state followed by eternal death. In reality, just the opposite is true. The phase of life we are now experiencing is limited to a relatively short span; then we will die. But more surely than spring bringing new life out of the dead of winter, more surely than dawn breaking from the dead of night, we shall rise again from our death into immortal life.

It is death that is the interloper in this universe, the temporary intruder, the unnatural state. The apostle John wrote near the end of his book of Revelation centuries ago, "God shall wipe away all tears from their eyes; and there shall be no more death, neither sorrow, nor crying, neither shall there be any more pain: for the former things are passed away." (Revelation 20:4.)

This fact makes all the difference in the world as we plan and carry out our activities here on earth. If we had only the short perspective of this brief life on which to analyze our actions, then we might be tempted to eat, drink, and be merry, for tomorrow we die. We might be lured into taking undue advantage of others, looking for the fast track to riches and the cheap success.

But what a sad and unfulfilling experience our lives would be! How we would desperately cling to youth and to life! If luck and fortune passed us by, we might well become bitter and resentful. Our later years would not be the serene acceptance of a life well lived, and the sweet anticipation of continuing on in another world. Old age would be the worried waiting for the knock of the grim reaper at our door.

Shakespeare, the master analyst of the human condition, described that view of life in the words of Macbeth. This general had betrayed and murdered his king in a ruthless bid for earthly power. But the prize turned to ashes in his hands. Macbeth summed up his outlook in these words: "Life's but a walking shadow, a poor player that struts and frets his hour upon the stage, and then is heard no more; it is a tale told by an idiot, full of sound and fury, signifying nothing." (*Macbeth* V, v. 17.)

This melancholy view of our existence might be accurate except for the sacrifice of the Savior of the world, which broke the bands of death forevermore. The empty tomb and the resurrected Christ changed the nature of existence for every person. The apostle Paul wrote, "As in Adam all die, even so in Christ shall all be made alive." (1 Corinthians 15:22.)

How precious is the promise of the resurrection! Without it, the burden of this life would be unbearable. A family I know recently lost a seventeen-year-old son. Handsome, talented athlete, a straight-A student, and an example of young manhood at its best, he was a son to gladden the heart of any parent, but his life was snuffed out instantly in a traffic accident. A young couple who had lost their first baby at birth were recently overjoyed with the birth of identical twins—but again, the babies lived for only a matter of hours. Another family I know plays quietly every day with their little son. He is a year and a half old, and the doctors say there is no cure for his illness. He will live only a few more weeks.

Sons who never come home from wars, mothers and fathers taken from their families, wise and loving grandparents passing on, and all of us destined sooner or later for the grave—what a cruel joke creation is if it is destined only for the dust. Who of us would dare to love or care for anyone or anything in this world with the specter of inevitable death and permanent separation hanging over every relationship?

But the word of our Father in heaven to us his children is sure and comforting. Death is but a temporary state. It is a passage from one stage of life into the next one. We shall rise again even as Jesus did. Well might we say with the apostle Paul, "O death, where is thy sting? O grave, where is thy victory?" (1 Corinthians 15:55.)

Section 2

OVERCOMING THE WORLD

13

How Do We See
the World?

James Branch Cabell once observed, "The optimist proclaims that we live in the best of all possible worlds; and the pessimist fears this is true."

An optimist is a person who sees a glass half full. A pessimist sees the same glass half empty. But which of them sees the real glass? That's an intriguing question. We accuse the optimist of seeing the world through rose-colored glasses. We suspect him of not being realistic, not facing the facts.

But as Sydney Harris reminds us, "In point of fact, all of us wear glasses of one sort or another. We all see the world, not as it is, but through the lens of a particular temperament and upbringing and angle of acuity. We put on these glasses at an early age, and rarely take them off, or even change the prescription as we get older."

Mr. Harris adds, "There is a profound difference between the glasses that are prescribed for us by the oculist and the ones we choose for ourselves. The oculist's glasses are 'corrective,' in the sense that they rectify our visual distortion and allow us to see the world more keenly and true. The glasses we put on for ourselves are exactly the opposite:

they distort the world to conform to our prior perception of it, and confirm our judgments of other people and ourselves." ("Seeing the World with Our Glasses," *Deseret News*.)

Yes, it isn't just the optimist who is looking through his own set of rose-tinted glasses. We all look through glasses of one hue, slant, or prescription or another. And when we accuse others of not seeing the "real" world, we only show how completely captured we are by the view we are getting through our particular lens.

In the most extreme and pitiable cases, these views are the outlooks of bigotry, prejudice, and narrow-mindedness. From there, the slanted viewpoint slips over the edge into neurosis, psychosis, and what we term psychological derangement. In many cases the mental patient standing with his hand in his shirt really does think he is Napoleon Bonaparte, and no amount of pointing out the world we see will make him believe he is not. These are extreme cases, but that is exactly the point. They are extreme cases of behavior that we all engage in to a lesser extent.

The world we experience is largely a construction inside our heads. This can cause problems for us and for the world, but it is also a great opportunity for us to create the kind of world we want to live in. We can see beauty all around us, for as Jean Anouilh has written, "Things are beautiful if you love them."

Many years ago a friend of mine was called to serve in the armed forces. He fought in several campaigns and saw many of his best buddies killed in action. In the process, he developed a hatred for the people he was fighting. The sight of them would raise his temperature and start his adrenalin flowing.

Then shortly after the war my friend was called as a missionary to return to this same country. He had a great internal struggle, but finally his better feelings conquered, and he developed a great love for the same people he had fought and hated. As this change took place in his heart, my friend said that a change literally took place in his eyes. The people who had once looked foreign and evil became the most beautiful people he knew. The people had not changed, of course, but my friend had. He had reconstructed the world inside himself. He had reground his perceptual glasses.

Even when we suffer misfortune, we have the privilege of deciding how we shall react to the people who may have wronged us. We can make them objects of our hatred or the focus of our concern, depending on how we see the situation. A few years ago a beautiful young woman was attacked on a dark city street. Her assailant left her bleeding on the sidewalk. As a final horrible act, he slashed her eyes so that she could never pick him out of a police lineup.

In the months that followed in her recuperation and return to as nearly a normal life as she could, this woman showed how beautiful she really was, inside and out. She refused to destroy herself with hatred against the man who had done this to her. She helped the police investigation, but only because she knew the man was sick and that this might be a way of getting help for him. She has continued her life of love and service to others, and through her blinded eyes she sees more clearly than most of us do with our so-called 20/20 vision.

Her story reminds me that there are some things in which we need not be twisted in our vision. We may never shake off the shackles of tradition, attitude, and personal taste that influence the way we see and interpret things of the world. Indeed, this individual perspective can be a blessing. Without the artist's unique way of seeing things, would we have the great masterpieces on canvas? Without the musician's interpretation of sounds, would we be without our symphonies? We need the optimist's rose-colored view of life when we are down, and yes, even the poor pessimist helps us balance our viewpoint and be more aware of the things in the world that need correcting.

People will always have differing opinions and outlooks on most things in this world. We need to recognize this, respect the interpretations and insights of others, and try to understand where they are coming from. We will probably never get rid of the glasses we are wearing, but we ought to at least be aware that we are wearing them.

There are some basic viewpoints in this life, however, in which we need not be confused. There is a way to get a clear and correct perspective on some vital questions. This way is through the guidance of God. If we ask him humbly, he will show us through his Spirit the most important things we need to know. We will see that he is our Father in heaven. We will see that every other person is also his child, and our brother or sister. We will find that this world was created for a purpose and that our individual lives are an important part of that purpose.

These and other basic truths we can know clearly and surely if we turn to him to guide our thoughts, our hearts, and our eyes. Perhaps this is part of what Jesus meant when he said, "The light of the body is the eye: therefore when thine eye is single, thy whole body also is full of light." (Luke 11:34.)

May we be filled with that holy light, and may his Spirit guide our eyes so that we may see each other as children of God and live our lives accordingly.

14

Whosoever Will
Save His Life

One of the most basic but most misunderstood teachings of Jesus Christ concerns losing one's life to save it. It is basic because the Lord found a number of ways to say it during his ministry. It is recorded in Luke, for instance: "Whosoever shall seek to save his life shall lose it; and whosoever shall lose his life shall preserve it." (Luke 17:33.) And in John, Jesus is quoted as saying, "Except a corn of wheat fall into the ground and die, it abideth alone: but if it die, it bringeth forth much fruit." (John 12:24.)

But though we have heard the concept often, it is still much misunderstood. How can one find anything, let alone himself, by losing it? The question is puzzling enough that our culture seems to have dismissed it altogether. Instead we are showered by appeals to the self. We are taught to be concerned about our self-development, and if we do that well enough, we are heading for self-actualization. Good old words like *fulfillment* and *esteem* have now become *self-fulfillment* and *self-esteem*. The question that haunts every self-scoring test and every television drama is "How can I make myself happy?" or "How can I find myself?"

We have been taught somehow to believe that life is

really a matter of survival of the fittest. Economically and socially we hope to outstrip our fellows, a dangerous premise for any Christian life. As one scholar noted, the United States is the only country he knows of where the adjective *aggressive* is used as a compliment.

Tom Wolfe described the 1970s as the "Me Decade" in an article reviewed in *Time* magazine. Amitai Etzioni, director of the influential Center for Policy Research, has suggested that the widespread search for self-fulfillment is crippling the family and the schools and, in general, corroding American life. He cites pollster Daniel Yankelovich, who found that 17 percent of Americans are deeply committed to a philosophy of self-fulfillment, and that ego needs and self-satisfaction take precedence over the needs of others, including family and spouse. Another 63 percent embrace the self-centered philosophy in varying degrees.

Among Etzioni's findings are that the emphasis on the so-called quality of life has brought a retreat from work and a widespread inability to defer gratification. He points out that the romantic educational philosophies of some have wrought an increase in unstructured classrooms where children are not taught the rigors of self-discipline, but are believed to be self-educators who can merely learn what they like. Etzioni mourns that in the age of ego, marriage has become not a lasting emotional commitment, but a breakable alliance between two self-seeking individuals.

But if Christ's teachings about losing one's life to save it are true, and I wholeheartedly believe they are, this self-seeking, self-centered mentality that has seeped into our culture is not only dangerous but also vain. We cannot find gratification by chasing it, nor can we find ourselves by constantly being on that search. Happiness and identity are by-products of a life involved in something bigger than itself.

Arthur Henry King said it this way: "We are told by the gospel the search for the self is not one which is undertaken in terms of the self, but outside the self and with others. The self is not self except in relation to others, in the family, and in the community. . . . Forget yourself, and you may become yourself. But if you think about becoming yourself, you will not have forgotten yourself and will, therefore, never be yourself." ("Are Mormons Joining in the World Suicide?" in *Sunstone* 7:3, p. 24.) What a paradox.

Phillips Brooks said, "How carefully most men creep into nameless graves, while now and again one or two forget themselves into immortality."

Think about it. The most miserable people we know are usually those who are obsessed with themselves. They have memorized their aches and pains, constantly rehashed their losses and disappointments, and learned to see every setting, every relationship in terms of themselves. "What do they think of me? What does this do for me?" become incessant questions. In fact, by and large when any of us have complaints, it is usually because we are thinking too much of ourselves. Life can never measure up when we are looking for perfect comfort, perfect control, and when every act is calculated to bring us some kind of tangible reward.

There once was a man whose neighbor, Mr. Hall, was in the same profession as he, and Mr. Hall was advancing far more rapidly than he. Mr. Hall seemed to have more money, and others came to seek him out and ask his opinion. This upset our man continually. He thought about Hall's success every day while he sat at work in his own small office. He felt overlooked and abused in his profession, and he became so miserable that finally even the quality of his work was affected. He couldn't think clearly about it; all that was really sharp in his mind was his own disappointment. "I'm not getting enough out of life," he moaned. "I deserve better. How can I change things for myself?"

One day, on a church assignment, this man visited another neighbor, Mr. Taylor. An elderly widower, Mr.

Taylor lived alone in an unkempt house because he had lost much of his sight and hearing and could no longer take care of himself. He had difficulty getting out to go grocery shopping, and he was dependent on neighbors who might remember to pick up a few things for him. He had been an avid reader, but he could no longer see well enough to read, nor hear well enough to enjoy books on tape. Without company, without occupation, every day was tedious and long for him, with no hope for a better tomorrow.

After his visit with Mr. Taylor, our man walked into his own home and saw it with new eyes. Here laughing children came to greet him; here were cleanliness and order, with lots of food in the refrigerator. He had important tasks to fill his hours and he had good health. Mr. Hall and Mr. Taylor were both his neighbors. Had he been looking out the wrong window all this time? Our man and his family determined to ease Mr. Taylor's life. They cleaned his house for him and did his grocery shopping. They took him on outings and visited with him often. The upshot of it all was that our man stopped concentrating on himself, and, when he least expected it, happiness came. It was a by-product of serving someone else.

Do we want to be happy? Do we want to find ourselves? Then we must give up the struggle and become anxiously engaged in a good cause that becomes more important to us than our own gratification. And we don't have to look very far for such a cause. As President Gordon B. Hinckley has said, "In any land, in any home, in any life, there are opportunities all around to stretch our lives in behalf of others." The Lord's promise to us is that if we will do that, we will find ourselves and great joy.

15

Looking Beneath the Surface

A friend of mine found an old chair that nobody wanted. It had sat in a shed, unnoticed, for many years, and when it was discovered again, it seemed like just another piece of junk, painted with layers of colors that revealed its history. But my friend likes to strip old furniture, and he took this chair on as a project. He thought that when it was stripped, it might be a nice little pine chair. He was wrong. Uncovered, it turned out to be golden oak, the kind of piece that made friends later ask, "Where did you ever get that wonderful chair?"

Those who like antiques soon discover, as my friend did, that appearances can't be trusted. The vase that is garnished with too many colors and fruits may in reality be worth a thousand dollars. The seemingly worthless 1940 comic book that has been lost in the basement may be a prize. And the furniture painted in garish shades may have its hidden glory.

Appearances can't be trusted. If you doubt it, consider one of civilization's oldest problems—forgery. Around the fifth century B.C., an Athenian poet was expelled from Athens for tampering with the oracles' work, and forgeries have continued since that time. Just a few years ago, in fact, the West German photoweekly *Stern* announced that it had come upon the astounding discovery of sixty-two volumes of Adolf Hitler's alleged diaries. Hailed by *Stern* as the "journalistic scoop" of the century, the diaries were quickly bought for serialization by other publications. The media buzzed with interest until experts began to take a closer look at the find. They were fakes, easily detected when the paper and ink were analyzed.

We have been hoodwinked again and again. In 1957, a mother and daughter offered to *Life* magazine phony diaries claimed to be Mussolini's. In 1971 a writer was able to convince McGraw-Hill publishing company that he had been charged by Howard Hughes to write his autobiography. The publisher paid him a fat $750,000 to begin the work. In every case the appearance was convincing, but it couldn't be trusted.

As in antiques and forgeries, so in life. We are often too quick to pass judgments on appearances. We are easily fooled by superficialities. Thoreau noticed this tendency when he wrote, "Let us settle ourselves, and work and wedge our feet downward through the mud and slush of opinion and prejudice and tradition till we come to a hard bottom of rocks in place which we can call reality. . . . Most have not delved six feet beneath the surface, . . . yet we esteem ourselves wise, and have an established order on the surface."

Thoreau suggests that most of us are content with superficialities, with merely seeming wise instead of really being that way. We are content to live on surfaces, respond to surfaces, and never think past them. How easy it is for important decisions to be based only on appearances. It is easy, but it is not safe, particularly in our human relations.

Appearances can have two devastating effects in our relationships. First, if we decide who is worthy of our time and attention only by appearances, we may pass by some of life's best treasures. Think about who the important others are in your life. Are they mostly just the people who had all the conventional trappings of success? Or are they just the people with whom you could easily identify? If so, you may have missed the gold. There may be someone you've dismissed without a second thought who could be a good friend, whose life embraces all that is noble about humanity, but who, lacking proper appearances, does not attract you. Would you have befriended the Savior, an itinerant son of a carpenter, who had no social standing? Would you have dismissed Abraham Lincoln, a dour, overgrown boy, the son of a rolling-stone father who kept him moving from one farm to another? Neighbors probably considered them a shiftless lot.

On the other hand, like the world duped by a forgery that seemed better than it was, appearances can urge us to esteem the shoddy, to value the example of those we should not follow. There are many weak characters dressed up as the rich, the powerful, the successful.

Second, trusting too much in appearances can magnify misunderstandings between people. I know of one mother who died, snatched before her time, and her four grown children all came back to their childhood home to bury and remember her. For each of them the grief was anguishing and unexpected, and many tears were shed. Two days after her death, as the children sat around the kitchen table eating the last cherry pie their mother had made, one of them remembered an incident with her from childhood that made them all laugh heartily. It was a release from the tension and grief of the preceding hours. But just as their laughter filled the air, two neighbors came to the front porch to pay their respects, and in the warm summer evening, with the door open, they heard the merry sound. Their eyes filled with shock and disbelief that this mother's children could be so heartless. They paid their respects curtly, left quickly, and never forgave the four grown children.

These callers judged from appearances and missed the truth of the matter. When we find fault, pick arguments, or criticize others, we ought to stop long enough to see whether we are only considering surfaces. The person who seems cold and aloof may only be tired. The person who seems irresponsible may only be overwhelmed with too much work. The person who is snappish and quick-tongued may only be discouraged. Before leaping to anger, before planting a silent grudge, we ought to take time to dig beneath appearances and be slow to judge. As in antiques and forgeries, so in human relationships. We must not trust appearances. Rather, we should settle in and work downward to a hard bottom of rocks in a place we call reality.

16

Forgiveness:
The Greatest Miracle

The Bible records many miracles in the Lord's dealings with his children. Joshua stopped the sun in its course. Moses divided the Red Sea. Jesus healed the sick, raised the crippled from their beds, and even brought the dead back to life. But in my thinking there is no miracle recorded in holy writ to surpass the miracle that can happen in the heart of each one of us through the power of forgiveness. Without forgiveness, civilization would have dissolved long ago in the poisonous acid of accumulated hatred. The saddest people in the world are those who let grudges and ill feelings canker their souls.

A friend of mine said he was awakened recently by a telephone call at three in the morning. The caller didn't even bother to identify himself or say hello or apologize for the strange hour. He immediately launched into a spirited recitation of the day's activities with his business partner. He began by saying, "Let me tell you what he did today." Then came a long and useless litany of the sins, evils, and injustices the man felt he had suffered at the hands of his business partner.

My friend wasn't totally surprised. He had endured

these emotional regurgitations before. He tried again to
show the man what was going on in his own mind. At the
very least the man was costing both of them a night's sleep.
But, of course, his problems were much deeper. His every
day and every night were dogged by thoughts of his chosen
enemy. He was wasting his valuable mental strength in
keeping track of big and little slights, affronts, and insults.
He was destroying what had been a beautiful and successful
business partnership. He was, in short, doing far more damage to himself than his partner or anyone else could have
possibly accomplished. The smarter thing would have been
to find a way to purge the venom from his system, because it
was slowly killing him. This would be good advice from a
counselor or a physician. The peptic ulcer he was putting together for himself might be a final tribute to the effect his
enemy had on him.

But there is much more to the principle of forgiveness
than just the healthful effect it has on mind and body. It is
one of the best medicines for the soul, and it is a prerequisite
to any progress we may want to make.

A family I know had been divided for two generations.
What started out as a spirited rivalry between companies
owned by two cousins had deteriorated into a barely covert
hostility between the family factions. It had smoldered for
years. But when my friend received a call to care for others
in his church, he felt that he could no longer harbor the feelings he had had for his cousins for so many years.

He went to the oldest of their family. He said it took
great courage and two tries. The first time his cousin was
not home. My friend was grateful and asked the Lord if that
wouldn't be sufficient. It wasn't. So he went back. Finally he
met in conference with his kinsman and confessed his feelings, and in the solemn and sacred moment that followed,
his cousin said, "I only wish I had been the one to come to
you." My friend said, "It doesn't matter who initiated it—

just that we have healed the wounds between our families."
And they wept together.

We can do little good work for ourselves or for others
so long as we harbor hard feelings toward those who have
trespassed against us. Part of the first and greatest com-
mandment given to us is that we love our neighbors as ourselves. The same goes for forgiveness. We must forgive our
neighbors, but it is just as vital that we forgive ourselves.

Jesus told the self-righteous and self-appointed pros-
ecutors who were ready to stone a woman in adultery, "He
that is without sin among you, let him first cast a stone at
her."

Even seething with hatred and pride as they were, this
mob could not deny the truth of Jesus' gently spoken accusation against them. The crowd melted away in shame. The
first half of the miracle of forgiveness had been started. But
then came the second step. The woman looked up, grateful
that she had been spared from death by the mob, but even
more conscious of her guilt and shame as she knelt before
this holy man who had seen her sins but saved her anyway.
We can have no doubt of the sincerity of her heart as she
turned her tear-filled eyes to him. This man who had saved
her from physical death would now show her the way to escape spiritual death as well.

He looked up from the ground and said, "Woman,
where are those thine accusers? Hath no man condemned
thee?"

She said, "No man, Lord."

And then Jesus gave her the blessed benediction that we
may all receive. He said, "Neither do I condemn thee: go,
and sin no more." (John 8:7-11.)

We are not told the rest of this woman's story, but one
cannot help but believe firmly that she went away cleansed
and renewed, and that, having been forgiven by others, she
found forgiveness for herself.

We may sometimes think it is humble or righteous on our parts to continue to mentally and spiritually flog ourselves day after day, year after year, for sins we have committed. But in a sense this is a denial of the mercy of God toward us. If he in his purity and righteousness can forgive us, who are we to not forgive ourselves?

A certain amount of sorrow is expected and appropriate as part of the repentance process. We will, by nature, feel remorse when we recognize we have wronged another or offended the Lord. And this is as natural as the fever of an illness or the inflammation and pain when we battle poison in our system. But after we have done all that we can to make restitution for our wrongs, after we have begged the forgiveness of all whom we have offended, after we have confessed our sins to whoever may be appropriate, after we have called upon the Lord for his forgiveness, then the time of fever and pain is over and the healing process, however slow, however lengthy, must begin. To deny this healing process is to deny the efficacy of the Lord's power upon us.

The miraculous healing of our souls through forgiveness is a constant reminder to us of the love of God. It is really the only way we can continue to make progress. As the apostle Paul wrote, "All have sinned, and come short of the glory of God." (Romans 3:23.) We would all be continually discouraged, downcast, and frustrated if we could not be forgiven for our errors.

Some people have asked me, "If I am forgiven of the act, why then doesn't it disappear entirely from my mind? Why do I still remember what happened?"

I do not know all the answers to these questions, but I do know a fine athlete who injured his knee. With proper therapy he has it back to where the doctors say it is as good as new. But my friend knows the movement that caused him his problem the first time. He doesn't do that particular move anymore. It hasn't hampered his game; in fact, I think he is a little better player than he was, because he has learned a couple of new skills to accomplish the same thing in the game without putting too much stress on his vulnerable knee. My friend is healed. He no longer feels the pain from his injury, but he does remember it, and he profits from the experience.

I don't know that we are promised we shall forget the wrong turns we have made in our journey of life, but we are promised that the memories will cease to bring us pain. And, if we are wise, we will use our experience to pinpoint areas in which we need to be careful so that we do not injure ourselves or others again. The promise is sure from the Lord himself that we can be purified, made whole again, and continue our journey back into his presence.

17

Reverence for God and His Creations

A girl who had just taken a walk in the woods was asked by Helen Keller, "What did you observe?"

"Nothing in particular," she answered.

"How is it possible," Helen asked herself, "to walk for an hour through the woods and see nothing worthy of note? I, who cannot see, find hundreds of things to interest me through mere touch. I feel the delicate symmetry of a leaf. I pass my hands lovingly about the smooth skin of a silver birch, or the rough shaggy bark of a pine. In the spring I touch the branches of trees hopefully in search of a bud, the first sign of awakening Nature after her winter's sleep. Occasionally, if I am very fortunate, I place my hand gently on a small tree and feel the happy quiver of a bird in full song.

"At times my heart cries out with longing to see all these things with physical eyes, but if I can get so much pleasure from mere touch, how much more beauty must be revealed by sight. And I have imagined what I should most like to see if I were granted the use of my eyes—even for just three days." (Quoted in David O. McKay, *Treasures of Life*, Deseret Book, 1962, pp. 394-95.)

We might all ask Helen's question. How is it possible to

walk in the woods and see nothing worthy of note, to pass through a day uninspired by some beautiful thing, to gaze blindly at a sunset? How is it possible? Because in our hurried lives we simply lose reverence for God and his creations. We have no time to look, and even if we look, no time to really see.

Yet, if we miss a chance to celebrate the earth, we miss one of the sources of nourishment in our hungry lives. Arthur Rubinstein once proclaimed, "Most people, in my opinion, have an unrealistic approach toward happiness because they invariably use the fatal conjunction 'if' as a condition. You hear them say: I would be happy if I were rich, or if this girl loved me, or if I had talent, or, their most popular 'if'—if I had good health. They often attain their goal, but they discover new ifs. As for myself, I love life for better or for worse, unconditionally." (*Reader's Digest*, December 1983, p. 193.)

What he says about life can be applied just as well to the earth, to natural beauty. When we say, "I'll love this earth if it's summer, or if the sun is shining, or if I'm in the mood," we put too many conditions on our enjoyment. We should love the earth and its natural beauty for better or worse, unconditionally. It was made to give us pleasure.

The Bible tells us that even the Lord himself, after each phase of creation, paused and called it good. And after making all these good things, he proclaimed, "Yea, all things which come of the earth, are made for the benefit and use of man, both to please the eye and gladden the heart." (D&C 59:18.) The earth can enliven us and give us pleasure if we will just open our eyes to it. Think of what Helen Keller would have yearned to see with only three days of vision.

The natural world can teach us deep lessons, too. When William Buchanan moved to Anchorage, Alaska, he assumed duties as chief of the Civilian Engineering Division of the Alaska Defense Communications Agency. That was a fancy title for a nuts-and-bolts job of maintaining a fleet of

B-52s across a tremendous, often icebound area with little more than baling wire and adhesive tape. In fact, the job was such a man-killer that after a few frustrating days and sleepless nights, Buchanan called in his deputy assistant, Ed Gallant, to set some priorities.

Gallant said, "May I suggest priority one? Let's go fishing."

"What?" exclaimed Buchanan, but that Saturday, they took to the lake, where Gallant led them to school after school of migrating salmon.

Buchanan was nagged by guilt not to be at his desk, but then came the lesson.

Ed Gallant sat down on a fallen log in a cove and pointed. "Look carefully," he said. "Just beneath the surface of the water are several huge salmon." Then he pointed to a ripple out in the channel where thousands of salmon were migrating upstream. He said, "They're fresh from the sea, and strong. But tomorrow they'll reach the Russian River Falls. They'll make desperate leaps up the face of the falls. Some of them will be too spent to make it, and they'll be dashed back against the rocks below. And then finally they'll die from sheer exhaustion."

He looked back toward the salmon in the cove and commented, "These are different. Some instinct has brought them to this quiet place. It's as if they know the falls are just ahead. Tomorrow they'll continue their migration, rested for whatever comes." (*Reader's Digest*, December 1983, p. 51.)

Suddenly priority one was obvious for Buchanan in his difficult new job.

The natural world can and should be a source of joy and growth for us. If it isn't, we need to train ourselves to be better observers. As one of God's creations, we are a reflection of him. Just as the poem introduces us to the poet, so the earth can teach us of God.

But with the privilege of being caretakers of nature comes a responsibility. In the simplest sense, it means we should never leave a place less lovely than we found it. We shouldn't litter or pollute. We shouldn't destroy animal life for mere pleasure. We shouldn't thrust a careless hand into the delicate balance of nature without understanding its consequences.

When David O. McKay was a boy, his dog killed a badger. "I carried the dead animal back to father," he said. "His face fell as I showed him the animal, and he said, 'Why did you let your dog kill it? It is a harmless creature, and there was no need to take its life. Who knows, it may even have some babies which now will starve to death in their hole!' I have never needlessly killed an animal since that time!" (*Home Memories of President David O. McKay*, comp. Llewelyn R. McKay, Deseret Book, 1956, p. 130.)

A modern prophet sums it up: "Men can not worship the Creator and look with careless indifference upon his creations. The love of all life helps man to the enjoyment of a better life. It exalts the spiritual nature of those in need of divine favor. . . . Nature helps us to see and understand God. To all His creations we owe an allegiance of service and a profound admiration . . . Love of nature is akin to the love of God; the two are inseparable." (Joseph F. Smith, *Juvenile Instructor* 53 [April 1918]: 182-83.)

18

Purging Pesky Habits

Most of us have a few pesky habits we'd like to get rid of—not the sort of thing that can get you arrested, just small irritations to ourselves or other people we care about. Little things like biting our nails or twisting our hair, talking too long on the phone, or being a little late for appointments. These habits don't amount to much, but in the sum total they can make a difference in our life success or failure.

I have a friend who is a very organized and well-informed accountant. He has great insight into financial matters, and his books are meticulously well ordered. But he has one problem. He is always late for meetings. It's not a big thing. The other people in the meetings smile and nod when he comes in five minutes after the appointed hour. But I'm sure that for a man as capable, organized, and well put together as he is, it must be terribly annoying to himself, and it must take away from his self-confidence and his effectiveness in every meeting to start out five minutes behind the eight ball.

I know people who make me flinch a little before I call them on the phone. They answer either with the piercing tones of a slave-ship commander or with a woebegone, simpering sound, as though there has been a death in the family. It wouldn't take a great effort to change their telephone manner, but it could make a big difference in how they are perceived by the person on the other end of the line.

As I say, I am not singling anybody out. We all have a few prickly places in our personalities. And most of us are interested in knowing how to get rid of them.

Dr. P. W. Buffington suggests these four steps for overcoming bad habits. First, work on one habit at a time. Second, discover what conditions, times, places, and even people reinforce or reward your habit and then avoid these. Third, select a new behavior you've been wanting and pair that old, powerful reward with it; for example, if you waste time on the phone because you love to talk, don't give up talking, just pair it with some habit you've been wanting to acquire, like jogging or teaching children to read. Fourth, narrow the cues that elicit that bad habit, and change those cues. If you bite your nails, put an elastic band on your wrist and snap it every time you bring your hand to your mouth. This will help change your reaction to this movement from pleasure to pain and help you break a nail-biting habit. ("Nasty Habits," *Sky*, July 1982, p. 36.)

Even the best of formulas and programs won't work if we don't; but if we really want to break a bad habit, we will. If we are just saying we ought to, however, we won't, no matter who else thinks we should.

The best way to get started working on a troublesome habit is to identify what it really is. It's probably not specific enough to say, "I'm always late." It is more useful to say, "I don't set my alarm early enough," or "I turn it off when it rings," or "I stay in a warm tub too long," or "I'm just not as fast at tying my tie as I think I am, and I need to allow another three minutes to do it." Whatever it is, pin it down as specifically and exactly as possible.

Now, find out when you're troubled with this pesky problem. If I overeat, is it at the dinner table, between meals, or late at night when the TV turns my mind to mush?

If I have an ornery disposition, am I grouchy all the time or just before dinner when I'm hungry? If you begin to focus on the problem, you may find you don't have to change your whole life, just a few troublesome times. That is a much less foreboding project than setting out to develop a whole new personality. Little pesky habits can hurt a person, but by the same token, small but good habits can be the key to great accomplishments over the course of a lifetime. And probably the best way to get rid of a bad habit is to replace it with a good one.

A friend of mine was a very successful teacher in college; then he went into the business world, became a prosperous salesman, and is now director of a company. People always comment on his enthusiasm. But he claims his success is largely the result of a simple habit. He said, "People talk about my enthusiasm. But notice where you get that idea." We thought about it for a moment; then he said, "My enthusiasm is 90 percent in my voice." He was right. He fairly bubbles when he talks from a lectern or to a class or a client. On the telephone his enthusiastic voice can lift your spirits for a whole day. He claims it's nothing more than a habit he developed years ago of using a bit more of his dynamic vocal range, a bit of breath control and diaphragm support, and putting his brain in gear before he starts his mouth into operation. Fairly simple skills, but they have helped make him a great success.

My wife and I were visiting some friends the other day. We always notice how sparkling clean their house is, even though they have a large family of young children. Yet our friends didn't seem particularly frantic about cleanliness, and their children were not hog-tied in the middle of the playroom as we might have supposed. As we visited with them, we noticed a little habit. Each of them subconsciously picked up anything that was out of place and put it away. As the husband took off his coat, it went on a hanger in the

closet, not in a pile on the sofa. His wife would inconspicu-
ously wipe up a smudge as she went by. Other than that,
they seemed like fairly normal people. But they had a habit
of keeping the things about them neat and orderly as they
went. A simple habit, but one that can make the difference
between feeling as though you are on top of your life and
your environment, and feeling as though you are constantly
reporting back to the outside world from the center of
a cyclone.

Little habits? Yes, but on them eventually hang the
biographies of men and the destinies of nations.

Charles Reade wrote, "Sow an act and you reap a habit,
sow a habit and you reap a character, sow a character and
you reap a destiny." There is real truth in this. People don't
usually end up failing or succeeding in this life by pure
chance. They make choices and develop habits along the
way that over a long period of time move them into this current or that in life's stream, and finally bring them to a certain destination, good or bad.

So don't let a few pesky habits stand between you and
the great person you were meant to be. Jesus said, "I have
given you an example, that ye should do as I have done."
(John 13:15.) Taking it one step at a time, we can follow his
example and become like him.

19

How Ethical Are You?

Many people think that if you try scrupulously to obey every legal and moral law these days, you must be crazy, addicted to some moonbeam philosophy of the past that used to work but just doesn't hold anymore. After all, they say, look around. Isn't it the con artist who is succeeding these days?

Not so, according to John Wannamaker, department-store mogul. He said, "Many persons have an idea that one cannot be in business and lead an upright life, whereas the truth is that no one succeeds in business to any great extent, who misleads or misrepresents."

Despite some evidence to the contrary, the bottom line is really that honesty does pay, that having a sound ethical basis to your life goes a long way toward making you successful in this world.

Now, the idea that right triumphs over wrong may be hardly new, but it seems important to assert it, and boldly so, in these days when honesty and personal integrity sometimes appear to be in short supply. And as we assert it, we have to remind ourselves that integrity and honesty have to be ours, right down to our smallest, seemingly most inconsequential act. Dwight Moody once remarked that "character shows—even in the dark." How true that is. Our true character is illuminated best when no one is watching.

Some college students went to a distant city one summer to find summer work, but they had a terrible time. Nobody wanted to hire an employee just for three months; employers were looking for permanent employees. One of them finally suggested that the students lie, say that they were looking for full-time work, and then leave at the end of the summer anyway. But one young person said that he couldn't do it. Yes, it may have been a small thing. Sure, he was far away from home and no one important to him would ever hear of it. But *he* would know he had done it, and some little part of him would be destroyed by the lie.

This young man discovered what it takes many much longer to learn. Whenever we don't perform at our highest ethical level, there is a loss in self-esteem. We lose some pleasure in looking at that person in the mirror. When we do not live up to our highest ethical standards, when a screw becomes loose in a machine, our parts stop working well together, and we really don't feel well.

William D. Brown, a clinical psychologist in Washington, D.C., put together an ethics test for *Success* magazine (December 1982) that is worth thinking about. Let me pose just some of the questions he asks in this test.

First, do you give a full day's work for a full day's pay? The lack of productivity among American workers has observers anxious on all sides. Someone somewhere is not working at work to his fullest capacity. Is that you? Some may believe they don't have to work hard at work because they don't like their job or they feel exploited by their employer. Are either of these good excuses? Absolutely not. It is as dishonest to goof off on the job as it is to take out of somebody else's pocket money that isn't yours. The temptation not to give a full day's work for a full day's pay may be one of the easiest to fall into. It is easy sometimes to chat instead of work, easy to slow down when a break or the end of the day is in sight. It is easy, but it is not right.

Second, asks Dr. Brown, do you ever take office items—even small ones for personal or family use? Pencils, erasers, and notepads have a way of disappearing from offices. One grocery attendant leaned over to another and whispered that he was going to call a long-distance sports-quiz number on his employer's phone. That is the same kind of thing. We can't rationalize that it won't matter if we take just one item home since the company has so many of them. That is not so. It does matter.

Third, do those who know you consider your word your bond—even your family? Do you keep your promises? Are you there when you say you'll be there? If you promise the family an outing or a treat, do you really pull through? Or are your promises, as Mary Poppins said, "pie crust promises—easily made and easily broken." Do you pledge things you don't mean, just to get yourself off the hook? In the end, these kinds of false promises put us on the hook as people learn not to trust us.

Fourth, would your friends describe you as a loyal and faithful friend to them? We all have bushels of acquaintances, but a friend is a rare commodity. That is because a real friend requires a commitment in time and energy. We have to be there to share joys and sorrows. And we have to be the kind of person another can trust with confidences. Can others let down their veneer of safety and share their vulnerabilities with you and know that you will love them just the same and it will go no further?

Fifth, do you strive to remain honest in all interactions both in and out of the office? Honesty is a habit that has to be acquired, like anything else that is really worthwhile. Let's face it—when we are tempted to be dishonest, it is often to save face. We want to appear better than we are. We want to pretend we've done the job. Or sometimes we simply want to make our lives more convenient. These are very human tendencies that we simply have to dispel from our lives. And when we want to teach this same principle to children, we have to remember that it starts with the smallest thing. We can't say, "Tell them I'm not here," to someone answering the phone for us and teach our children honesty in the next breath. It just doesn't work.

Sixth, if your spouse's emotional and physical fidelity were equal to yours, would you be satisfied? Let me tell you what Brown says about this: "Days of the 'double standard' in marriage are gone for good, and thoughtful men and women will say 'Good riddance!' It is important for both sexes to recognize that fidelity underscores commitment, without which a relationship couldn't survive." Emotional fidelity is just as important. Each of us must learn to put the needs of our spouse above all other things, and not let business or other people supersede that relationship.

Seven, do you really treat others both at home and away from home the way you want to be treated? It is sometimes easy for us to be polite and charming to people outside our homes, but are we as good to the people who live there? Do our families ever receive the benefit of our courtesy, our good cheer? It is essential that they do.

And it is also important to treat the stranger we will never see again with the courtesy we would shower upon our most influential friend. Think about how you treat other drivers on the street, someone who wants the same parking place you do when it's the last one on the block, the clerk at the store when you are in a hurry.

These questions bear very strongly on our personal integrity, and our integrity bears very strongly on our personal success in this life. Virtue is not only its own reward; it rewards us in tangible ways every day we practice it.

20

Be Honest with Yourself

On the fourth day of a recent National Spelling Bee, 85 of the 137 contestants were eliminated, including Andrew Flosdorf. The word that got him was *echolalia*, "e-c-h-o-l-a-l-i-a." When Andrew had spelled it, he had mistakenly substituted an *e* for the first *a*. The judges misunderstood him and thought he had spelled the word correctly.

It wasn't until after the round that some of Andrew's friends asked him to spell his word and he learned of his mistake. He gulped back his tears and went right to the judges, who had to eliminate him. It was hard to do, but Andrew said, "I didn't want to feel like a slime."

The chief judge of the event, Robert Baker, said, "We want to commend him for his utter honesty." So did the world, it seemed. Suddenly the thirteen-year-old was besieged by reporters requesting interviews and appearances on network television. Andrew was surprised by all the attention. "The first rule of scouting is honesty," he said.

But we live in a world that gives attention to rare events. The old journalistic saw is that it is no news when the dog bites the man, but if the man bites the dog, start the presses. Honesty, especially when the stakes are high as they were for Andrew, has become rare enough to make the news. Unfortunately, we have become conditioned to dishonesty. "Lie a little here. Cheat a little there. It's okay," too many say. "Everybody does it."

The day that everybody really does do it, we are in big trouble. If America ever falls, it won't be because a better system has developed. It will be because our system has become overburdened with dishonesty and laziness. As Paul Harvey said, "We don't need new religions, we don't need new ethics. We don't need a new system; we need only to make honest the one we have."

Where did we get the creeping attitude that nothing is wrong with dishonesty? When did it become fashionable to cheat on taxes and pad expense accounts? It's time we turned it around or pay forever for the consequences. History teaches us that people eventually get what they deserve.

In fact, entire nations have been subverted by dishonesty. I know of one couple who lived in a certain third-world country where dishonesty was so common that friends and relatives could not mail them packages at Christmas. Boxes intended for them would be broken open and the contents stolen before arrival. When they shopped for food, they couldn't trust the labels. So-called fresh-frozen chickens had often been sitting on the docks for days in the sun and then refrozen to sell. At home, household help lifted their watches and silverware without a twinge. Dishonesty was almost a custom—and a miserable one. They said they learned to feel always insecure, slightly unsafe, guarded about their possessions, and worried to find what would be missing the next day. "Well," the people of the country said, "everybody does it."

There are some things that everybody ought not to do, and the place to start in making a change is with ourselves. Would we be perfectly satisfied living in a world where our neighbor is exactly as honest as we are? Or would we suddenly find ourselves more wary of lending possessions, accepting checks, counting on promises? We can expect no better from people than we are willing to give. We must lead our lives by a standard we consider acceptable for all, not find excuses why the rule shouldn't apply to us. Each of us should keep in mind that when one person repents, there is one less rascal in the world.

Most of us feel good about what seem to be the big issues. We haven't robbed any banks lately, or swindled our company out of millions, but do we feel as good about the so-called smaller issues? Check your library shelves. How many books there belong to somebody else, borrowed and then forgotten? Look at your bills. Are any of them past due for services already rendered, goods already in your possession? Consider your taxes. Have you taken only those deductions allowed and strived to pay your full share? Look through your desk. Are there any supplies there that were pilfered from your job with the excuse, "Oh, what's a little pen after all I've given them"?

I've often wondered, when it comes to cheating and lying, if there are any little things or little issues. The smallest wedge can penetrate the psychological barrier against dishonesty, and once broken, it is easier to break again until dishonesty is a habit. We may even abandon it eventually as an ideal. If that ever happens, individually or collectively, our quality of life will drastically slip. Dishonesty does not pay: it always costs.

Hi Nelson wrote a story about a boy named Jack who found out just how much it cost. "One more test and I'm finished—graduated!" thought Jack.

He shuffled into the last seat in the corner. It was cooler there. The window was wide open, and every now and then, when he felt like resting his mind, he could look out and daydream.

"He had little to worry about," Nelson wrote. "He had studied hard. Besides, his marks had been high all term.

"Test papers were passed out and then the last nervous

chuckles and jokes came to an end. Just then Jack noticed Ted Zorens. He was sitting right across the aisle. As Jack tackled the first few questions, he glanced over at Ted now and then. Jack could tell that Ted was in trouble. Obviously he hadn't studied for the exam, but that was not unusual. He was so good at spotting the answers on the other students' papers that his friends called him 'Obie,' short for 'Old Binocular Eyes.'

"Jack could hear Ted's fingers tapping nervously on the desk top. If Ted flunked this exam, he wouldn't graduate. But luck was with him. A girl student on the other side of the room was sick. The pressure of the exam was too much for her. She had been too nervous to eat breakfast that morning. Now she felt faint.

"As the teacher called an assistant for help, Ted made his move. He passed Jack a note: 'Just list the twenty short answers.' Jack hesitated only an instant. Ted was his friend. No one was caught; no one was hurt. Ted graduated.

"Jack lost touch with Ted after graduation. Not until fifteen years later were they to meet again. Jack was a salesman. He had been driving for eight hours straight. He fell asleep at the wheel and his car slammed into a tree. Jack was barely conscious as the ambulance screamed through traffic. The stretcher-bearers rushed him into the operating room for surgery. He heard the voice of the surgeon. 'Don't worry, you'll be fine. I'm Dr. Ted Zorens.'

"As Jack went under the anesthesia, he could hear the nervous tapping of fingers." (Source unknown.)

Who needs a cheater at a time like that? Who ever needs one? May we all be heroes of honesty like young Andrew Flosdorf!

21

Reaching Out to Others

A few years ago, a little girl named Fern attended high school in a small town. It was the tradition in this school to recognize every year the student who showed the most school spirit and support for the basketball team.

Fern was not a candidate for the honor. She was not a candidate for any honor. She was one of those nice but unnoticed kids who don't become much but a face on a yearbook page and a name on the rolls. Actually Fern had barely achieved that status. Her family was poor, and they lived out of town. She was not part of the in crowd, and the only time her name came up in a conversation of other students was in that mocking, sarcastic way that seems funny when you're young, insecure, and need to ridicule somebody else to take the pressure off yourself. Her name became synonymous with anything dumb or out of style. If a thing was unacceptable or ridiculous, the students called it "Ferny."

Kids can be so cruel.

So at the high school games as at everything else, Fern usually sat alone.

Then the final assembly came, and the students were prepared to honor that student who had showed the best school spirit. Sure enough, they called out the name of one of the more popular girls on the pep team. She bounced up the aisle, full of smiles and waving to all her friends. But then a little miracle happened. She took the stage and said, "I can't accept this award. Yes, I have loved the team and cheered for them at every game. But Fern has come to every game, too. I came in a nice warm car surrounded by my happy friends. She usually came alone and walked all the way, two and a half miles, sometimes in the rain or snow. She had to sit by herself, but I don't know anybody who cheered with as much spirit as Fern. I would like to nominate her for the most enthusiastic student in our school."

Fern was escorted to the stage to a spontaneous standing ovation from her fellow students.

Kids can be so kind.

Fern is a mature woman today, her hair streaked with gray. Many things have happened to shape her life, but nothing more important than that outburst of acceptance and appreciation from her friends that memorable day. I submit to you that there are mature men and women today who can't remember how many games that team won or lost that year, but who have never forgotten and will never forget the warm feeling they had when they stood up and cheered for Fern and welcomed her into their friendship and society.

Reaching out to others is not an easy thing to do, particularly when you're young. To take the hand of another at the risk of your own popularity takes a mature and Christian outlook indeed.

But how desperately we need that kind of caring in our world today. "Positive peer group pressure," as the social scientists call it, may be the salvation of this generation. Young people today are being hit on all sides by subtle and open attacks on their ideals, their morality, their faith, and their self-confidence. At the same time their traditional support systems of family, church, and school are eroding. It is no wonder that alcoholism, drug abuse, immorality, and crime are rising at alarming rates.

But there is a brighter side to this gloomy picture. Though thousands of young people are struggling and falling in the battle of life, others are winning in spectacular ways. Young men and women are accomplishing things today that we used to assume it took a lifetime to do. In science, literature, the arts, and social, civic, and other important work, we can point with pride to millions of talented teenagers who have set lofty goals and are going to attain them. The question is, how can we help those who are stumbling to lock arms with those who are striding confidently up the road of life? I heard these words of wisdom recently from a young woman named Marianne Mortensen. Let me pass them on to you. She said:

"Most of us have a difficult time resisting those who have a genuine love for us. Such people have a way of becoming important to us because we know we are genuinely important to them. The cry of youth today is for authenticity, for genuine concern, and for meaningful relationships with our peers. . . . Of a meaningful relationship I would think immediately of the Golden Rule, 'Do unto others as you would have them do unto you.'

"For teenagers, that is a difficult thing to do. Charity for those outside of our circle of friends is difficult to comprehend when we feel so comfortable within the confines of our 'group.' But if we look at the life of the Savior [we] see that he didn't leave his 'group,' the apostles, or the love of those friends about him. He merely opened his arms to all who would listen. He increased his fold. So . . . we do not have to leave our groups to learn to care for the feelings of our peers. We just need to open our arms and increase our friendships. Developing faith and righteousness would be a key to lighting a flame within ourselves that would shine as a guide and a blessing to those around us. . . .

"We should be desirous always to respect the feelings, the ideas, and the desires of others. It should be a commitment to accept people for what they are and not what we would have them be. This does not mean that we accept sin and evil, but that we recognize that each person has different life experience and a different reaction to that experience. We need to live and build, basing all on the teachings of Jesus Christ." (Talk given at the Lancaster California Stake conference, April 17, 1983.)

Marianne Mortensen was right on target. The teachings of Jesus can be our guide as we try to reach out and befriend those about us. He welcomed followers from every walk of life. He was often criticized for associating with sinners and outcasts. He reminded his critics that it is not the well who need a physician, but the ill. As the great healer of souls and bodies, he went among those who needed him. We should attempt to do likewise.

But though Jesus went among the spiritually ill, he did not succumb to their sicknesses. That is also something we need to remember. The best service we can render those who are struggling in life is to offer them a good example to follow and a strong arm to lean on until they can get on their feet.

22

Humor—God's Bright Gift

Have you had your laughter quotient today? That may sound like a frivolous question, but humor is something we're going to discuss seriously for a minute. It is probably the most underrated, most effective way of dealing with life's rough moments. As Gordon Owen said, "It can be used for patching up differences, apologizing, saying 'no,' criticizing, getting the other fellow to do what you want without his losing face. For some jobs it is the only tool that can succeed."

Why? I think it is because life is basically a hazardous affair, and if we become too solemn about it, we can crumble. Too often we lose because we have bared our fists against a problem and mounted a frontal attack, when a touch of humor might have helped us win.

Humor can stop a misunderstanding from escalating. Its power here lies in the unspoken premise, "You let me off the hook, my friend, and I'll let you off." A husband and wife had a fight as she drove him to the airport. He felt miserable, and he knew she did too. Two hours after she returned home, she received a long-distance phone call. The operator said, "Person-to-person for Mrs. I. A. Pologize. That's spelled 'p' as in . . . " Suddenly the whole day changed from grim to lovely at both ends of the wire. ("The Crying Need for Laughter," *Royal Bank of Canada Newsletter*, February 1979.)

Humor can build flagging community spirit. It has been said that next to the heroic British RAF, British humor did the most to fend off a German takeover of England in World War II. One sample: "The story is told of a couple fleeing in their night clothes to a bomb shelter while their block was being flattened during the Blitz in London. They had scarcely reached the street when the woman turned to go back into the imperilled house.

"'What are you doing?' shouted the Cockney husband.

"'Have to go back. Forgot my false teeth,' she said.

"'For heaven's sake,' the husband cried above the din of the falling bombs, 'they're not dropping sandwiches, you know.'" (Ibid.)

Humor can buoy us in personal crisis. By this I don't mean the canned humor that comes from jokes and comic routines. I don't even mean that when things are rough we should try to look on the light side or "laugh it off." Instead, humor is the ability to appreciate the ridiculous and incongruous in our own experience. It takes courage and intelligence to recognize our own foolishness and deflate our own pretensions. But when we operate with a sense of humor, we look at ourselves and our troubles with a wider perspective. As one writer said, "We see our own predicaments and our own adversities in the broad beam of the floodlight, rather than the narrow beam of the spotlight. And that makes each predicament a little less serious. Developing a sense of humor will not eliminate the problem, but it will help us overcome the negative effect on our own physical, mental and emotional well-being." (Spencer J. Kinard, "The Spoken Word," September 12, 1982.)

In fact, a simple rule of life is that many so-called crises plus enough time yield humor. That is why prosperous people in their mid-life will talk about days of student poverty with fondness or a woman will recount with such hilarity her first ruined meal as a bride. Recently I heard a woman laughing about having fallen in a manhole when she was eight months pregnant and spending days in bed to recover. Was it funny at the time? No way. Now it is her favorite funny story.

As Earl Wilson said, "Even get-well cards have become so humorous that if you don't get sick, you're missing half the fun."

None of us would ever like to admit we didn't have a sense of humor. In fact, essayist Frank Moore Colby said, "Men will confess to treason, murder, arson, false teeth or a wig. How many of them will own up to a lack of humor? The courage that could draw this confession from a man would atone for everything." And yet we don't have a sense of humor if we can't laugh at ourselves. Laughing at others takes no particular insight, but seeing our own foibles is a real art.

Adela Rogers St. John tells the story on herself of receiving a Bible from her granddaughter for her eightieth birthday with the wish, "Grandma, I just wanted to help you cram for finals." And Conrad Hilton, the hotelier, was asked on national television if he had one vital message for Americans. Turning to the cameras, he said, "Please—place the curtain on the inside of the tub." (*Reader's Digest*, December 1983, p. 119.)

We love to laugh and we need to laugh to deal with that deep vein of melancholy that runs through everyone's life. The airwaves are leaden with attempts to make us laugh. Millions of dollars are spent annually on situation comedies, silly game shows, and stand-up comics to make adults do what comes naturally to an infant who chuckles at the sight of a falling stack of blocks. That ought to remind us that the best laughter is that which erupts naturally in the everyday course of events. And there is a lot of it. Life is at least as funny as it is sad. And when it is sad, the best way to cope is to flex the muscles around our funny bone. The next time we are in a tight spot, we should ask, Can I handle this with humor?

23

So Much
to Be Thankful For!

The year was 1943. A U.S. Coast Guard ship slogged through the southern Pacific Ocean carrying supplies for embattled troops on an island outpost. On the ship the men went about their duties, but their thoughts were far from the open ocean before them. Many of them thought of the turkey and traditions and Thanksgiving Day back home. One young seaman in particular was lost in thought, standing at the back of the ship. It was hard not to be pensive and even morose at a time like this. It wasn't the turkey and stuffing he missed. In fact, he had had enough of that to last him a while, for he was a cook on the ship and had prepared thousands of turkey dinners that day.

No, it was the idea of Thanksgiving that had set him thinking deeply. What had he to be thankful for? And how should he show his thanks? He looked at the rolling clouds overhead and the flat sea stretching in all directions. The symbolism of distance was hard to escape—distance from others, and from the Lord, and sometimes he even seemed to be estranged from himself. What should he give thanks for, and how should he give thanks?

But then suddenly an idea struck him. His face brightened. A warm smile crossed his face and lit up his eyes as he turned and quickly went to his bunk on the lower deck. He took out a pen and began to write. These words would be read by his family and a friend. A few years later from that same man's pen would come words that would be read by the world. For the young seaman's name was Alex Haley. And the book he would write, entitled *Roots*, would inspire us all to remember how much we owe to others, particularly our families.

But this time he was writing simple letters of thanks to people who had helped shape his life. As Alex Haley describes his reasons for gratitude, they were not earthshattering, not that much different from all of us. His father had been a teacher at a small college and had not neglected to teach his son a love of language and ideas. His grandmother had given him love and discipline when he needed it and helped him grow up straight. And the Reverend Lonual Nelson, who had taught Alex and the other little pupils in a humble school, had begun each day with a prayer to God for them. Alex never forgot. ("Thank You," *Parade Magazine*, November 21, 1982, p. 4.)

Like many of us, Alex Haley had taken a while to notice that his life even in adversity was a cornucopia of blessings spilling over. Each of us could make a similar list of blessings, blessings that many times we do not recognize or acknowledge.

I know a father and mother who are determined that their family will not let the little blessings slip by unnoticed. Every night before they go to bed, the parents ask their children, "What was the best thing that happened to you today, your happiest thing?"

These little children, like most of us, can often build a heartbreaking tragedy out of a broken shoelace. It's not uncommon for them to say, "Nothing good happened today." And so these parents and children have a dialogue something like this:

"Did you wake up this morning?"

"Uh huh."

"Did you get out of bed?"

"Well, sure."

"A lot of people didn't, people who are sick or crippled. Did you see the sun come up? Did you go out and feel it warm on your skin?"

"Yeah."

"Blind people didn't see the sun. Deaf people didn't hear the birds sing. Did you have breakfast?"

"Sure, we always have breakfast."

"Most of the world started the day out hungry, and they will go to bed hungry again tonight. Did you have a new idea today, and did you tell somebody about it?"

"I guess so."

"There are a lot of places in this world where you can't have a new idea and just go out and do it. You have to ask the authorities. But we can. That's part of being free."

It doesn't take too long for the children to get the idea. Unfortunately, it also doesn't take most of us too long to forget the other idea either.

Centuries ago a prophet counseled his people to remember to give thanks to the Lord who gives us everything. He went on to tell how indebted we are to the Lord and always will be; that even as we draw a breath to give him thanks and gratitude, that same breath is a gift from him. (See Mosiah 2:19-25.)

Some time ago, we all watched the courageous battle of Dr. Barney Clark as he became the first recipient of an artificial heart. He was a brave pioneer who helped push back the frontiers of knowledge and skill in preserving life. At his bedside were the finest doctors, supported by the latest equipment. Ultimately all this skill, research, money, and knowledge were focused on one function of the body, keeping a heart beating. For weeks they held out against the encroaching power of death. But finally, death came despite their best efforts.

I never think of Barney Clark and his courage nor the doctors and their dedication without touching my chest and being just a little amazed. Without so much as a second thought from me, my heart continues to pump life-giving blood hour after hour, day after day, month after month, and year after year. How much have we to be grateful for?

I suggest that right now you touch your heart; then look at the fingers that allowed you to feel the beats. Look at the complicated muscles and tendons that make the incredible hand work. Think of the eyes that allowed you to see that hand. Think of the brain that directed your thoughts there, and the thoughts inside your brain—the memories, the warmth, the love. Think of those who share that memory space with you, who have given you a smile or a kind word, or created something beautiful for you to enjoy. Think of those who have shown you a great example to help make you what you are. Think of the hundreds of thousands of little acts for which you are indebted to others.

Think of the privilege of being alive on this earth.

When Jesus cast evil spirits out of a man, according to the Bible, the spirits asked permission to enter into the bodies of a herd of swine. They entered the swine and immediately the animals rushed down a hill, over a cliff, and plunged into the sea and were drowned. (See Luke 8:27-33.) I don't understand all of the implications of that story, but one thing it tells me is that having a body and life to make it work must be a very precious possession indeed.

May we then get back to basics. Let us, for a time at least, pause in our aspiring and struggling to obtain more or get more or do more, and give gracious, heartfelt thanks to those who, like Alex Haley's father, grandmother, and teacher, have helped us become what we are. And most of all let us give gratitude to the God who gave us life and all that we possess, even our latest breath.

24

Aging: It's All in How You See It

We live in a youth-oriented society where the best advice we can give is something like I saw on a poster advertising a craft class: "Get Grandma off her rocker. Sign up for ceramics."

We don't know quite what to make of growing older each day. In fact, a job-seeker was filling out an application blank, but when she came to the line that said, "Age," she hesitated a long time. Finally, another job applicant seated next to her leaned over and whispered, "The longer you wait, the worse it gets."

You don't even have to wait that long for it to be bad, according to newspaper columnist Twila Van Leer, who wrote, "You may have noticed. Nobody pays any attention to middle-aged people. . . . The middle-aged person loses all identity. To the government, he's a taxpayer; to the kids, he's an open wallet; to the community, he's up and coming but not yet arrived; to the young, he's too old to be with it; to the old, he's too young to be venerable."

She complained, "If a kid forgets his lunch money five days in a row, he is excused on grounds that he's too young to know better. If Grandpa goes out in public without his

teeth, he is benignly excused on the premise that the aged
are entitled to their little idiosyncrasies." ("Middle Age Is a
'Funny' Place to Be," *Deseret News*, October 21, 1982.) But
middle-aged people can claim neither innocence nor forget-
fulness.

For all we joke about aging, in reality the richness or
poverty of life at any time depends on our maturity, which
for most of us increases with our experience and time in life.
Oh, there are some losses that come with time, but the ad-
vantages far outweigh them. This is because there comes the
moment when all our mirrors turn into windows. As one
person has said, "That is the moment of growing up. The
adolescent looks inward; the adult can look outward," and
finds that the world is much bigger than the right package
he makes in himself. (*Reader's Digest*, February 1963, p.
262.)

I believe that the great asset of maturity is that we come
to know ourselves and feel comfortable about what we find.
An important part of growing up is to learn to accept ourselves as we are, without trying to be what we are not. None
of us are as skilled as we'd like to be. We may not have the
talents or money or flash of our neighbor, but the mature
person can handle that, recognizing individual differences
as part of life, and even rejoicing in them.

The mature person is not deceived about his own limitations. He knows there are plenty, but it is only from this
understanding that one can move forward. The mature person is willing to expose his ignorance by asking questions.
He does not need to pretend he already knows. The mature
person dares to try his talents. He is not afraid of failure, recognizing that it is part of every success. The mature person
can even learn to laugh at himself, because he sees that he
has the human foibles common to us all. For the really mature person, life may become less solemn as he grows older.

"The Greek playwright Aristophanes caricatured the

philosopher Socrates in his drama *The Clouds*, and all Athens roared with laughter. Socrates went to see the play, and when the caricature came on the stage he stood up so that the audience might better enjoy the comic mask that was designed to burlesque him. In that action he gave an evidence of his maturity." ("On Being a Mature Person, *Royal Bank of Canada Newsletter*, December 1977.)

Not only does a mature person learn to live significantly for himself, but he also lives significantly for others. One writer pointed out that "he develops from the stage of thinking 'Please help me,' through 'I can take care of myself,' to 'Please let me help you.'" (Ibid.)

A mature person weighs the consequences of his actions, not just for himself, but for others. He does not live by the law of the jungle, fighting tooth and claw for some kind of supremacy. Instead, he recognizes that he is part of a family and a community—a whole network of relationships—people whose well-being may depend on what he does. In fact, the mature person progresses to the point where what makes someone else happy will make him happy too. If someone else errs, he can accept that, knowing that he has erred himself. He can take others' shortcomings in stride too. His center is so well-grounded that very little will knock him off balance.

"One of the fatalities of our culture," said H. A. Overstreet, "has been that it has idealized immaturity. Childhood has seemed to be the happy time." The truth is that years bring a wisdom and perspective about life that is real happiness. "The young may build themselves imaginative castles, but as part of their maturity, they learn to take off their coats, go into the quarries of life, chisel out the blocks of stone, and build them with much toil into the castle walls." ("On Being a Mature Person," *op. cit.*) To believe that youth is better than age is to value the dream over the achievement. May we not be so foolish as the years pass by.

Section 3

OUR FAMILY
SUPPORT SYSTEM

25

The Functions of a Family

I know of no other social institution with so much potential for good as the family. School, counseling center, first-aid station for the body and soul, financial center, haven of the oppressed—all these and much more, the home and family can serve.

For example, we pay thousands of dollars for education, but nothing affects the academic success of a person more than the environment in his home. A mother reading to a child on her lap can do more good than innumerable hours in a school remedial-reading program.

We spend untold sums visiting counselors, psychiatrists, and therapists to keep our heads on straight and our minds at ease. But nothing can soothe the troubled soul like having a mother or a father or sometimes a son or daughter listen to us as we pour out our hearts. There is no finer therapy obtainable in the world.

Often we respond and recuperate from illness better with love and concern and comfort in a family setting than we do in a hospital. Though the hospital may have superior equipment and a better trained staff, they cannot duplicate the feeling of being among our loved ones. Recent research has indicated that just getting a hug can help us be smarter and healthier.

Over the past several decades in America, we have seen people struggling to find meaning and purpose in their lives. There are, of course, many ways to spend one's life well, and much good work that needs to be done, but nothing is more important than the work we will do within the walls of our own homes. David O. McKay once said, "No other success in life can compensate for failure in the home."

Does it seem to you that if a home could do all these things, it must require a bit of care, maintenance, and organization? Take any of those areas—education, health, welfare, or finance. Any institution set up to serve even one of those human needs would require a considerable staff, a fairly large capital investment, and a lot of work. Yet many of us go along week after week, year after year, assuming that somehow our family will muddle through with almost no attention.

It won't. We as a nation are finding out how serious the consequences can be when we turn our eyes from the homefront, our most vital line of defense against the troubles and the dangers of the world.

But if a family requires constant attention and care, this certainly need not be a drudgery, only if we make it so. Think back on your own happiest memories. How many of them were tied to family activities? If I may, let me just sketch out a week's worth of things a family might do.

On Monday, we could get together just to enjoy each other's company, to share a good book or stories or experiences, sing a few songs, work a puzzle, play a few games— just have a good time together.

After we have done this for a few Mondays and the shock of being around each other has worn off a little, we can set some individual and family goals and feel the great satisfaction that comes with making progress. This is a fine time to praise each other and remember how much we need and love one another. And speaking of remembering, we should remember to bring refreshments. It's miraculous what a few cookies can do for any occasion where families are involved.

Oh, and just one note of caution. There is one member of the family I would exclude from these activities simply because he is obnoxious. He monopolizes the conversation. His remarks are often insipid and boring and out of place. Yet for some reason he commands more attention than is due, and he usually takes the best spot in the living room and is the focus of much care and attention. Often eyes and ears are riveted on him when more important people go unnoticed. This obnoxious member of the family is the television set. Let's leave him out of our family-evening activities. We won't miss him, believe me.

Tuesday might be a good night to consider communications. Let's listen to the words that fill our homes. Are they soft and soothing, or harsh and grating? Almost any knotty problem will eventually come unraveled if we can talk it out. And let's remember that the other side of understanding is listening. It is an indispensable part of communication.

On Wednesday we might want to think about helping each other feel special. Each of us is a champion, and if we don't appear that way, it is only because we haven't found our game yet. Again, it is miraculous what a few minutes talking and listening to our children at bedtime can do. And it's marvelous how a weekly date can restoke the fires of love between a husband and wife.

Thursday could be a day to count our blessings. One good way to recognize and remember these is to write them down in a diary or a journal and enjoy reading through it. We might also take a look back where we came from, and gather pictures and stories of mom and dad, grandma and grandpa. These can give our families a greater sense of solidarity and continuity.

Friday might focus on finances. We can get the whole

family involved in setting goals and saving for things we each want. Most of us find resources and abilities we never thought of when we put our heads and hearts together as a family.

Saturday can be a trial or a treat. For many families, Saturday is the day when the parents would like to clean up the house and the yard. But to the children, Saturday is that glorious brief moment of freedom from school, a day whose patron saint is Huckleberry Finn. While there is much worthy work that needs to be done by families, it's important also to remember that the family that plays together stays together.

But it takes praying as well as playing to keep us all pointed in the right direction. Sunday is a particularly good day to remember this. There are so many things we need to do or want to do in this busy world that it is sometimes easy to forget our most important opportunities and obligations. Our obligation is to remember the Lord and to keep his Sabbath day holy. Our opportunity is to join in a partnership with him in keeping those we love together in happiness and harmony. Regular church attendance and prayer can be a big step on the journey we all want to take together.

These are just suggestions, of course, and they would need to be adapted to each family. I offer them here with a prayer that each of us will catch the vision of what a heaven we can make of our homes both here and hereafter.

26

Fairy Tale Endings

"And they lived happily ever after." This is the phrase that ends most fairy tales. The prince and princess have overcome hardship to find each other, and the rest is magically easy. There is no more to the story. Marriage is anticlimactic after the romance of courtship. We know better. In reality, the wedding day is not a final destination, but the place where the adventure really begins.

The Most Reverend Robert Runcie told of a real-life prince and princess, Charles and Diana, at their marriage: "On a wedding day it is made clear that God does not intend us to be puppets, but chooses to work through us, and especially through our marriages, to create the future of his world."

Marriage is a new creation for the partners themselves. As husband and wife live out their vows, loving and cherishing each other, sharing life's splendors and miseries, achievements and setbacks, they will be transformed in the process. A good marriage is a life, as Edwin Muir says,

> *Where each asks from each*
> *What each most wants to give,*
> *And each awakes in each*
> *What else would never be.*

So nobody just lives happily ever after. Fairy-tale endings are created by two people who work hard at it and are never the same again for their efforts. That is because real love learns in marriage what "happily ever after" never knows.

First, real love is realistic. A scene with two sweethearts silhouetted on a beach walking hand-in-hand into the sunset is dazzling, but people don't live together that way, except on vacations. Rather we see each other in the harsh glare of every day, where warts and pimples, wrinkles and sags are all too evident. Nobody could hide their faults in marriage even if they tried. Marriage reveals us for what we are—not that perfect, romantic image, but somebody who sometimes stumbles and often wouldn't send anyone's pulse racing. Real love accepts that fact and doesn't go dashing off in search of someone else, because life isn't always like a romantic novel. The mundane here-and-now can bring great joy if we don't place unrealistic expectations on it.

Second, real love doesn't expect us to be mind readers. Too often couples expect their partners to intuit their moods and needs, and they feel stricken when that doesn't happen. Mind reading may be a good magic trick, but it is more than we should ask of our marriage partner. Yet we fall into that trap frequently.

I know of one marriage in which the husband and wife have very different attitudes about birthdays. He hates any fuss made over him and is embarrassed by cards and cakes. She, on the other hand, counts on the fuss and is sentimental about the cards and small remembrances. You can foresee the trouble. Every year on her birthday, her feelings are hurt because he treats her just as he wants to be treated—no fuss. She expects him to know just what she would like, and he always fails dismally. He's not very good at reading her mind.

Well, neither are any of us. We can't expect our mates to

read our minds. We have to tell them how we feel and learn to be direct about our feelings and desires. Partners often stumble and fall over unspoken messages.

Third, love knows that it can't make life painless. We ask too much of our partners when we expect them to give us everything we ever missed in life, or even if we expect them to totally understand us. We don't understand ourselves that well, so how can we expect someone else to know us so well they can anticipate our every need and compensate our every failing? How can we expect such undaunted perfection from them that they will accept our every weakness unconditionally? If there is ever something missing in our lives, we ought not to blame our partner, but search ourselves. Nobody else should ever be responsible to make us happy. That is our own job. Real love knows that.

Fourth, real love knows that it doesn't matter who is right. Too many quarrels are caused because partners try to prove they are right. The issue can be petty or great. Often it doesn't matter. When one is out to prove he or she is right and the other is wrong, no one will win.

One marriage counselor reported that couples often asked him to judge who is right or wrong in certain situations, when many of the issues presented are matters of personal preference rather than those that are intrinsically right or wrong. "Both partners are right in the way they feel," he said. Feelings cannot be argued; they can only be accepted or rejected.

"Partners get in trouble when they fail to separate thinking from feeling. There can be no arguing about the way they feel, while ideas can be argued. Emotions are tied to self-esteem, and expressing understanding of another's emotions is the beginning of psychological equality. How important is being right to you? Have you learned to allow your companion his or her feelings, even though you disagree, perhaps even violently, with the opinion expressed?

Bonds are strengthened when couples can accept each other's feelings without being threatened. A mate is allowed angry feelings, differing opinions, other friends, or occasional thoughtlessness." (Herbert G. Zerof.)

Finally, real love knows that marriage is a commitment. It is not just a garment to be tried on to see how it fits and then discarded. A young starlet was being interviewed about her future plans, and she said that she'd like to get married sometime, and she'd probably be divorced sometime, too. "Everyone does," she shrugged. One can almost predict the success of her marriage with that kind of attitude.

I contrast that with the commitment of an older and wiser woman who, married a second time, was reflecting back on her first marriage. "Now I know we could have made it, if we'd tried a little harder. This marriage is working, not because my husband is better than my first, but because now I know what it takes."

When people live happily ever after, it is because they know what it takes—faith, perseverance, and real love. The welfare of our world and the growth of each individual hinge on this kind of marriage.

27

Feelings of Love

John Powell told of this experience: "It was the day my father died. In the small hospital room, I was supporting him in my arms, when . . . my father slumped back, and I lowered his head gently onto the pillow. I . . . told my mother, 'It's all over, Mom. Dad is dead.'

"She startled me. I will never know why these were her first words to me after his death. My mother said: 'Oh, he was so proud of you. He loved you so much.'

"Somehow I knew . . . that these words were saying something very important to me. They were like a sudden shaft of light, like a startling thought I had never before absorbed. Yet there was a definite edge of pain, as though I were going to know my father better in death than I had ever known him in life.

"Later, while a doctor was verifying death, I was leaning against the wall in the far corner of the room, crying softly. A nurse came over to me and put a comforting arm around me. I couldn't talk through my tears. I wanted to tell her: 'I'm not crying because my father is dead. I'm crying because my father never told me that he was proud of me. He never told me that he loved me. Of course, I was expected to know these things. I was expected to know the great part I played in his life and the great part I occupied in his heart, but he never told me.'" (*The Secret of Staying in Love*, Niles, Illinois: Argus, 1974, p. 68.)

Love is not just a way of feeling; it is letting others know how we feel. A puppy could have the greatest love for his master, but the master would never know if the dog didn't wag his tail and prance about his feet when he came home. So it is with people. What makes us so sure that those we love know it? Even God himself took the time to vocalize his feelings when he said, "This is my beloved Son, in whom I am well pleased." (Matthew 3:17.)

Why don't we share our feelings more often with those we love? One reason is that we become absorbed in our own problems. Sure we appreciate our family and friends, but we are so preoccupied that there seems to be no energy left to express our love. We just hope they'll know. Anyway, we are sure there will be time later to say and show how we feel. But strange as it may seem, life doesn't slow down. Something will always preoccupy us. A problem will always be pressing. The old story is often repeated about the wife who always wanted an orchid corsage and finally got it—on her coffin. Jesus did better in his relationships. We know that in his hour of anguish on the cross, he looked down and beheld his mother weeping there, and he forgot his own pain long enough to assure her that John would take care of her. We must express our caring for others despite our problems. Life will never present a better moment than now.

A second reason we may not express our feelings is that we take our loved ones for granted. This is especially true in marriage. A man, for instance, may think his wife looks pretty, but he will neglect to tell her, thinking she knows he thinks so. "She ought to know," he might say to himself; "I told her so twenty years ago."

Sometimes we become numb to the good performance or the special efforts of those closest to us. We just expect it, forgetting how much thought and energy go into each good action. Those closest to us are most dependent on our sympathy and appreciation. We can't forget that. I know a parent who had two sons. The first was a consistently excellent student. The second hit a high only once in a while, but when he did, his father loudly praised him, hoping to encourage more of the same. Finally the first son asked the father why he never earned that same praise. "Oh, I just expect it of you," answered his father. We may expect good performance from our loved ones, but let us not take it or them for granted.

A third reason we may not express our feelings of love is that we are too busy with criticism. Ask many children if their parents love them. "Are you kidding?" they will probably say. "All they do is tell me what I do wrong." Every parent knows what a responsibility it is to rear good children. I believe it is that very weight that makes parents critical. Our child is sloppy or argumentative, and we justifiably want to nip that failing right in the bud. The problem is that growth is a long, slow process, and we need to appreciate him right where he is. If a child hears nothing but criticism from his parents, it may be hard to convince him it is motivated by love. "Your room is messy. You always procrastinate. Why did you do that?" Even before children have arrived at some point the parent finds acceptable, they need to be told they are loved. They need lavish praise for their good efforts. Loving words should always outweigh critical ones in a parent-child relationship.

The fourth reason we don't express our loving feelings is that we are afraid. We may think sharing our love and appreciation for someone is an admission of weakness. We are above that, certainly beyond the need for it ourselves. That is not true. Nearly everyone we meet is hungering for sympathy and appreciation. Let's give it to them. We do not need to be afraid.

Loving means making a conscious effort to notice the

good things others do and then telling them about it. One woman in a marriage enrichment course was asked to go home and compliment her husband on something good he had done. She went home and looked at him. He spent most of his time around the house watching TV; he was irritable much of the time; she just couldn't think of anything on which to compliment him. "Go try again," the instructor told her the next week in class. "If you can't find something to compliment him on now, search your memory until you find something." The woman searched her memory and finally found something. "Have I ever told you how much I appreciate all the hard work you did during the Depression to keep our family secure? I really appreciated that," she said. Suddenly her husband started to cry. He had been needing someone to notice something good about him for a long time.

Loving means building up others every chance we get. I watched a violin teacher work with a young student. The student made awful, screechy sounds on the violin, but the teacher seemed not to hear it. "You take such beautiful long bows," she said.

Loving means appreciating others where they are, and it means saying it. "I love you. You matter to me." John Powell would have given anything to hear these words from his father. They beat all the Valentine cards in the store.

28

Lessons about Love

Not long ago Mike and Catherine Hauk of Terry, Montana, went dancing. Like Eliza Doolittle in *My Fair Lady*, they "could have danced all night." And they did dance more than five hours. He looked deep into her eyes and she into his as they swayed gently to the music. They were in love and everybody knew it. But nobody but themselves knew how deeply in love they were.

Oh, the townsfolk had some idea, and those who heard them repeat their marriage vows earlier in the evening were no doubt impressed with their sincerity to love and keep and care for one another in sickness and in health. But even they couldn't know how much Mike and Catherine meant what they said. For the sparkle-eyed couple in love were repeating promises they had made to each other back in 1912. Among those watching this seventieth wedding anniversary ceremony were seventy-one children, grandchildren, great-grandchildren, and great-great-grandchildren.

The family and friends dried their eyes, shook hands all around, and then Mike took his Darlin' dancing as he had 'most every Saturday night since this century was barely a decade old. (*Deseret News*, October 18, 1982, p. A-2.)

Mike and Catherine can give us all a lesson in love. In our fast-and-fancy, hurry-in-and-hurry-out, free-and-easy, do-your-own-thing society, we have developed strange and sometimes selfish notions about what constitutes true love. We have given each other the mistaken idea that there is really only one kind of romance: the white-hot flame that streaks like an electric arc between two people who share some magical mix of conductive chromosomes. Fiery, uncontrollable, master of every other thought and feeling, wild and untamed—this is the love we sing and write about. And when it doesn't happen, or the electric tingle settles down a bit, we grow disappointed and wonder where the romance went.

In reality, love is much more like a growing, living plant than an explosive, bursting fire. It needs gentle sowing to begin with. It then needs fertile soil and a proper climate in which to grow, and like any worthwhile and beautiful thing, it takes time to flower into its most nearly perfect form.

This is a lesson that needs repeating over and over again today. In our fair land, where almost half of the people who love each other enough to take the vows of matrimony later find themselves in the pain and misery of a divorce court, we apparently need lessons in love.

These people did not set out to deliberately hurt themselves, their chosen mate, children, and others who got caught and ground up in the heartrending and stomach-wrenching pain of divorce. They loved each other once. That's why they got married. But they let their love starve. They did not nourish it and continue to care for it so it would grow stronger as they needed it. A fire will grow cold without fuel. A plant will wither without nourishment, and love will die if it is ignored.

Dr. Paul E. Dahl, a marriage counselor, gave the following seven assignments to help us keep the love in our marriage. (See *Ensign*, July 1982, pp. 56-60.) I commend them to you.

Assignment number one: Strengthen your relationship

with our Father in heaven. Richard Lovelace wrote a poem that ends with these famous lines, "I could not love thee, dear, so much, / Loved I not honour more." ("To Lucasta on Going to the Wars.")

The same might be said of love for our Father in heaven. We can love each other more when we love him. As we learn to love and serve the Lord and his children, our fellowmen, we grow and mature into more unselfish and caring individuals. Then our love for one another in marriage becomes a beautiful, mutually growing relationship and not a sad story of two selfish and sick souls clinging together for support against the world.

Assignment number two: Spend time together. Somebody commented on the old adage, "Absence makes the heart grow fonder—for somebody else." In this busy world of appointments, meetings, schedules, and assignments, don't forget to schedule some time for the most important person in your life. What is sadder than to see a husband and wife who, when the dust has settled from the hectic pace of career and children, look at each other across the breakfast table and see almost a stranger sitting there?

Assignment number three: Listen to each other. Remember this good piece of advice. You have two ears and one mouth—use them accordingly. Nowhere is that more important than in marriage.

Assignment number four: Develop a friendship with your spouse. Does that sound strange? I wish it were. Unfortunately this is a step in love that we often overlook. But a friend is one you like to be with, share your inner thoughts and feelings with. You think of a friend's needs even before your own, and you value a friend's opinion. Friendship is a solid foundation upon which to build and maintain a beautiful edifice of love.

Assignment number five: Do something special for each other every day. This doesn't have to be a dozen long-stemmed roses or breakfast in bed. A phone call, a love note in a lunch box, or a specially thought-out compliment can cover a multitude of mistakes and even an occasional forgotten anniversary.

Assignment number six: Share new and special insights and experiences. Here again, this doesn't have to be Paris in the springtime. It can be the sunset from your back porch or a book from the library. It's the sharing, not the size of the adventure, that counts.

Assignment number seven: Take a second or third or fourth honeymoon. Get away from the rest of the world for a little while and remind each other why you fell in love. You will probably find that true love, like great music and literature, grows deeper and more profound with time. Each time you return to it, it seems to have an added luster. The notes or the words have not changed, but we bring deeper understanding and appreciation to what was always there. Let your love grow into this, and it will never turn old and stale.

And when the going gets a little rough, take each other in your arms and remember Mike and Catherine Hauk dancing through three-quarters of a century.

29

"All Those Endearing Young Charms"

Thomas Moore's wife lay alone in her room. The darkness about her was oppressive to those who came in, but to her it was a comfort and a shield. The fastened shutters and tightly drawn drapes emitted no light from the outside world. She wanted none, for with light would come sight, the sight of her disfigured face. Where there had been beauty, there were now only horrible scars of smallpox. No one must glimpse her face again, she thought, especially her husband. He, the sensitive poet, the lover of beauty and fine things, had loved her in her beauty. He would be revolted at the sight of her now, and she would not blame him. Only the darkness could protect her. But even as she thought these hopeless thoughts, she knew he would soon return from his business trip.

The latch on the door turned, and her heart sank within her. The door quietly opened, and in the subdued light from beyond the room she saw his silhouetted form, the man she loved with all her heart but who could never love her again.

He spoke her name softly, gently. She did not reply. He entered the room, closed the door, and went to the windows to pull the drapes.

"Please don't," she said. "Please leave me as I am. Go and never return."

After a moment he left. Downstairs in their home, he prayed all night as he searched his heart and his mind for the right thoughts, the right feelings, the precious words that would carry his deepest meanings.

Thomas Moore was a well-known Irish poet of the nineteenth century. He had written many fine and popular verses, but never before had he so wanted to express his love and understanding. He had never written a song, but this time only a melody could carry his message.

In the morning he returned to the darkened room. "Are you awake?" he asked.

"Yes," she said, "but you must not see me. Please don't press me, Thomas."

"I'll sing to you, then," he said. Thomas Moore then sang to his wife the song that still lives today.

Believe me, if all those endearing young charms
Which I gaze on so fondly today,
Were to change by tomorrow and fleet in my arms,
Like fairy gifts fading away.

He heard a movement in the corner of the darkened room where his wife lay in loneliness. He continued:

Thou would'st still be adored as this moment thou art,
Let thy loveliness fade as it will,
And around the dear ruin each wish of my heart
Would entwine itself verdantly still.

The song ended. As his voice faded, Moore heard his bride arise. She crossed the room to the window, reached up, and slowly withdrew the shutters, opened the curtain, and let in the morning light.

And thus came about one of the greatest love stories in

literary history, and one of the best-loved songs ever penned, "Believe Me If All Those Endearing Young Charms."

One reason this song has endured through the years is that it is founded on fact—the fact that true deep and abiding love is not the explosion of emotion that most popular songs describe. Real love is not founded on a pretty face and a comely form. Real love, like real beauty, is not skin deep; it is soul deep. And both love and beauty grow as we serve one another.

That is why mothers are so beautiful and why they become more beautiful with each passing year. My own mother has grown too lovely for a camera to really capture. Any chemical imprint on photographic film can only dimly reproduce the inner light of love that shines from her face. I thought she was the prettiest mom on the block when I was little, but it has taken me a good part of a lifetime to realize how exquisite she really is. I feel like Walt Whitman when he wrote that he was "well-begotten, and raised by a perfect mother."

Was Whitman's mother perfect, or was mine? No, not really, and that is a point that needs to be made. Some mothers (my wife among them) have told me they are uncomfortable on Mother's Day because they can't live up to the idealized supermom we describe in stories, songs, poems, and greeting cards. But that is just the point. Perfect, unmarred, and unmarked statues are not mothers. Nobody could cuddle up to a chiseled marble representation of motherhood. Mothers are struggling, imperfect people like the rest of us. How could a mother empathize with a skinned knee if she herself had never stumbled?

It is this continual striving to improve, this lifetime of effort to be a good example, that turns a pretty girl into a beautiful, mature mother and a serenely radiant grandmother. The endearing young charms become enduring beautiful virtues. These virtues do not fall on a woman, even a mother, automatically with the passing of the years. They are the fruits of strenuous and dedicated service.

The old saying is that a mother's work is never done. It is also true that her influence is immeasurable. Her actions help shape the minds and mold the character of her children and her children's children to untold generations.

Tennyson describes a noble hero in his poem "The Princess":

Happy he
With such a mother! Faith in womankind
Beats with his blood, and trust in all things high
Comes easy to him, and though he trip and fall,
He shall not blind his soul with clay.

Thus it is. The beauty of a good mother goes beyond her own being. It is largely because she has shown us beauty that we can find beauty in the rest of the world, and because of her trust in us that we can trust in others and be trustworthy ourselves. And it is her love and confidence in us that helps us have the strength to rise when we fall and to try again.

30

What to Give Mother

An intrepid and resourceful reporter pretended he was delivering a package to get past the doorman. Once inside the house, he found his interview as difficult as he had anticipated. The dour, wrinkled woman was vehement in her denunciation of Mother's Day. It was a commercial sacrilege, and she wanted no part of it. All of the merchants were greedy, she said, but the florists and flower peddlers were the worst of the lot, hawking their white carnations like so many money changers in the temple. Unable to get a single cheery word for the holiday from her, the reporter bade the bitter old woman goodbye and left to file his story.

Who was this Ebenezer Scrooge of Mother's Day? None other than Anna Jarvis, the woman who had given most of her life and all of her fortune to establish Mother's Day in America and forty-three other countries. But the selling of gifts for mothers had so disillusioned her that she was sorry she ever started the custom. (Oscar Schisgall, "The Bitter Author of Mother's Day," *Reader's Digest*, May 1960, p. 64.)

Miss Jarvis must have been doubly displeased to see the founding in 1941 of the National Committee on the Observance of Mother's Day, an organization dedicated to promoting commercial interest in the occasion. By the late

1950s, these entrepreneurs had edged out Easter as the second biggest buying holiday of the year.

It's too bad Miss Jarvis had to spoil the best years of her life over the matter, but she did have a point. The sweet, sentimental song of mother doesn't sound quite the same when it is played solo on a cash register. Besides that, mother can present a problem on Christmas, Mother's Day, and her birthday. By the time many of us are old enough to seriously consider what kind of gift she might appreciate, she already has the usual stuff we think of as presents. There isn't much on the store display rack that will make her eyes twinkle. She has collected most of the paraphernalia we people gather about us. More importantly, she has realized that beyond a few basic necessities and comforts, most of our possessions need to be cleaned, oiled, serviced, and adjusted, and are in truth more trouble than they are worth.

And so mother falls into the problem area of gift giving, those who are "hard to buy for," who have everything. But do they really?

I sometimes wonder if Ralph Waldo Emerson's mother would have had happy Mother's Days? Surely she would have, if that wise philosopher followed his own counsel. I have no reason to believe he didn't, for Emerson gave us the key to real gift giving when he said, "The only gift is a portion of thyself." That is all any of us has to offer that is really special. Most of the goods for which we give our lives in this world are cut out of a pattern, pasted from a plan, or mass-produced from a mold. About the only unique things around are people and snowflakes. It is difficult to give a portion of a snowflake, so that leaves just a bit of us to give back to Mom on her day.

Certainly if there is anyone who would appreciate the uniqueness in us, it would be that mother who counted our toes and fingers when we first came into this world; who could recognize our cry of discomfort and pick us out from the chorus of wailing wigglers in the hospital. It would be the mother who pored over our class picture until she found our funny first-grade face; who recognized the rasp in our breathing in the night and got out the steamer for our croup; who bathed our bodies, probed our minds, and listened to our fears, our complaints, and our little brags and moments of triumph.

To our mother, each of us is a rare and unique wonder of the world. We are the Taj Mahal, the Hope Diamond, the Grand Canyon, every singular and irreplaceable treasure of the world, all rolled into one.

Erma Bombeck, that witty and articulate mother and newspaper columnist, had a word to say about this situation. She wrote, "Children sell themselves short. They think they have nothing of value to give. They are wrong. 'How about lunch? I'm buying' is equal to one Rolls-Royce with ultrasuede fenders.

"'I'm not going anywhere tonight. How about a game of Scrabble?' is worth a ruby pendant surrounded by a cluster of diamonds.

"'I can only stay 12 hours, but I wanted to spend Christmas with you and Dad,' is worth 200 acres of the Grand Canyon.

"'Let's get a live tree and trim it together,' is worth a private car on the Orient Express.

"'I love you' doesn't even have a price. It's invaluable.

"The older you get, the less you are impressed with material things. They are dust catchers that you thought would love you back, but they don't. These are tough times for young people who must be anguished about what to get the generation that 'has it all'—something that doesn't have an exorbitant price tag. How about giving a part of yourself? It'll fit without any alterations. It will match any decor. It'll be something they don't already have and they won't take it back to exchange. Trust me." ("Gifts for Parents Who Have It All," *Deseret News*, December 1982.)

This might be the year to give a bit of our time, our concern, our heart in place of those flowers that will soon wilt or another kitchen appliance that needs to be cleaned. This year, let's get down to the heart of things, for that is what mothers are made of.

As in all aspects of our life, we may take our pattern from the Master. Jesus was always concerned about his mother's welfare. He looked to her needs and cared for her concerns. On the cross, where every breath was a stabbing pain and every word a groan of agony, he used his last remaining strength to make provision for his mother weeping at his feet. "Behold thy son!" he said to her as he placed her in the care of his disciple John. To John he said, "Behold thy mother!" (John 19:26-27.) And John took her into his home and cared for her. Such was the concern of the Lord for his mother. May we partake of that same spirit at all times!

31

A Father's Greatest Work

Let me reintroduce to you three seemingly successful men. The first held an important religious post in his community. He was privileged to enter sacred buildings that others could not. He performed his duties well and faithfully all his days.

The second was even more prominent in religious affairs and was, in fact, a prophet and a judge. He received the rod of the Lord for his people and helped to direct their religious and even their temporal affairs. He was a strong and a fearless leader and did much good.

The third was a successful king and general. His reign is remembered even after many centuries as the high point in the history of his people. His leadership was legendary and his beautiful poems are treasures of literary chronicles. He was a multitalented man, a dynamic leader, and his subjects loved him.

Most of us would be hard pressed to match the records of these men. Yet I said at the beginning that these three men were seemingly successful. Take nothing away from them. They were great men, served well, and were honored and will be blessed for their fine work in the world. But they shared a common heartache. Their children chose evil over good.

The dedicated priest was Eli, who served in the temple of ancient Israel. Eli carried out his religious duties faithfully, but he did not teach his sons to honor the Lord. The results were disastrous for his family. His sons Hophni and Phinehas were part of a panic-stricken rout in battle that cost Israel its treasured Ark of the Covenant. Eli fell to the earth, broke his neck, and died when he heard what had happened. His daughter-in-law, Phinehas's wife, went into premature labor at the shock of the news and died in childbirth. It was a pitiable end to what could have been another righteous generation in a fine family. (1 Samuel 4:17-20.)

Because Eli's sons were unworthy, the youthful Samuel replaced them as priest and judge of the people. He served long and well, but ironically, when it came time to pass on the judgeship to his sons, they too were unworthy. The Bible records they had "turned aside after lucre, and took bribes, and perverted judgment." (1 Samuel 8:3.)

So disgusted were the people with Samuel's sons that they threw out the whole system of judges and instituted a royal line of kings. This proved to be a serious mistake in matters of state and of the spirit. And again, one of the reasons was the revolt of a son, the fair-haired and smooth-tongued traitor Absalom. The rebellion failed, and as Absalom tried to escape on a mule, his beautiful long hair became tangled in a tree and left him hanging helpless before the swords of the pursuing soldiers.

A disinterested reader might note that Absalom got what was coming to him, and then turn the page. But any father would be gripped by the anguished cry of King David when he heard the news that Absalom was dead. "And the king was much moved, and went up to the chamber over the gate, and wept: and as he wept, thus he said, O my son Absalom, my son, my son Absalom! would God I had died for thee, O Absalom, my son, my son!" (2 Samuel 18:33.)

In the heart of a true father, nothing brings a deeper sorrow than the sins of his son. But no sin can make him reject and cast off his child.

These great men of the Bible offer us another testimony that no work a man does is as important as the care and teaching of his children. Fathers, our sons will look up to us. We will be a force in their lives whether we are present or absent. Whether our example is good or bad, we will teach and lead our children in one direction or the other.

Yes, fatherhood is a sacred title and responsibility. I hope that all of us privileged to serve in that position feel that responsibility firmly on our shoulders. But having said that, I hope the seriousness of the work doesn't scare us off or cause us to feel incapable.

None of us are perfect fathers or supermen. We know this. The Lord knows this, and, thank heaven, even our children know this. They are all willing to forgive us, to work with us, to help us as long as we are doing our best to be decent fathers.

We are all a bit like the old farmer who met the young county agent along the road one day. The enthusiastic young agricultural adviser said to the old timer, "You should have been to the meeting last Saturday. We learned all kinds of new and better ways to farm." The old farmer thought a minute, twitched the straw in his teeth, and said, "Well, I reckon that's so, but I ain't farmin' now near as good as I know how."

Most of us probably ain't fatherin' now near as good as we know how, and perhaps the last thing we need is more instruction and theory on how to go about it. We all know in our heart of hearts the thing we could be doing to better bless the lives of our children. I don't particularly want to hand out any new recipes; I want just to emphasize how important we are to the most important people in our lives, our wives and children.

But let us also remember that we are not the only force. Other influences are at work as our children find and follow the courses they take. Ultimately they are free human beings just as we are, free to decide whether they will do right or do wrong, free to follow the higher or the lower road through this life and life to come. We cannot drag them to success in this life or to heaven in the next. We would not want to. We must learn to let them lead their own lives and make some of the inevitable mistakes that all of us must make in the process of growing and learning and developing in this life. That can be terribly painful, but there seems to be no adequate substitute for experiencing life firsthand.

Each of us will eventually account for our own actions. We cannot take the full blame for the mistakes of our children nor the full credit for their successes. Likewise none of us can blame our parents if we turn out to be something different than we hope. And so if our children are giving us pain and grief as parents, part of that comes with the territory and the job. We cannot become disheartened. We cannot quit. Ultimately there is only one way to fail as a father, and that is to stop trying.

May we never stop trying to be good fathers. May we catch the vision that no worldly success or honors can compensate for failure in our homes. May we try to help the few sick souls among us who are abusing their wives and children. May we keep trying when it seems to all the world that we have failed. Prodigal sons still return long after we may have been tempted to give up hope. A celebration and a fatted calf, an open door, and open arms are the best things we can keep in readiness for that blessed event in a family.

Above all, may we pattern our fatherhood after the example given to us in the holy scriptures and whispered to our hearts by the Holy Spirit. May we look to our own most loving parent, a personage whose accomplishments defy our description and even our understanding, who commands galaxies, whose power and knowledge and abilities are greater than we can comprehend, who in all his glory and majesty could have been called by the most magnificent titles the tongues of men could devise. In his love and concern, patience and empathy for us in our struggling mortal state, he has told us to address him as our Father in heaven. I pray that we may always do so and emulate his example.

32

Preparing for Fatherhood

What man among us has not sometimes dreamed of having a beautiful young girl put her arms around his neck, look into his eyes, and say, "I love you. You are the most important man in my life." Who of us has not wanted to be some combination of Socrates' wisdom and Superman's strength to the admiring eyes of aspiring youth?

These dreams and many more are fulfilled every day for good fathers. To a little girl, for a time at least there is no man in her life so special as daddy. For a young man looking for a model for his actions, words, and thoughts, there is a time when nobody can do it quite like daddy. What a privilege, what a blessing, what an opportunity it is to be a father!

And what a responsibility it is, because the other side of these delightfully true daydreams is the nightmare of a father who doesn't fulfill his destiny, who fails and forsakes his own flesh and blood. What man could live with himself if he saw those same trusting eyes grow wretched, empty, despairing, and wasted, and know that he was the cause? Who of us could bear the accusing voice of pain and disillusionment stabbing us in the heart, saying, "Dad, if it had not been for you, I might have made it"?

The stakes are just that high in this serious and sacred

work of men which we call fatherhood. Somebody once said of athletics that it is easier to become a champion than to be one. The same is true of fatherhood. It is much easier to become one than to be one. Most physically healthy males can beget offspring, but to be a real father is a commitment of a lifetime. It demands and it brings out the best in a man. Whatever other responsibility he carries is secondary to the one he has to his own children. New presidents can be elected; new chairmen of the board can be chosen; new athletes will rise to wear the laurel crown. Scientist, doctor, professor, general—all of the lofty titles men aspire to are temporary and can be assigned to someone else. But the designation of dad is permanent. Every child has only one. And despite what we may choose to think, a man's influence on his child is forever.

Dr. Daniel G. Brown, a family counselor, wrote, "When men fail as fathers, whatever success they may be in other respects, including eminence in their profession, they have failed in life's most serious and sacred trust." ("The Psychology of Fatherhood," *Vital Speeches of the Day*, September 1, 1961, p. 704.)

In this world of sometimes twisted values, men may spend decades preparing for a career. They may spend a lifetime struggling to reach the top in their profession. Yet they sometimes spend almost no time preparing and very little time performing some of the most important duties they will ever do—fatherhood. A few years ago studies showed that out of 168 hours a week, the average man spends about seven and a half minutes teaching, talking to, or listening to his children. That is a little over a minute a day. Who of us would expect to succeed in any endeavor in which we applied ourselves for one minute a day? You can hardly brush your teeth in that little time.

Time and timing are both important in raising children. A few moments spent at the critical turning points of a teenager's life are worth more than years when the child has grown to adulthood and his life patterns are solidly set. The brief and vital fleeting moments must be captured in their proper time, or they may never come again.

There are times in all boys' lives when they are reachable and teachable. Many things must happen at the proper time and in sequence, or the plan is frustrated. At this critical time in boys' lives, they need but will not demand love or attention; either they receive genuine love and attention or they go without. When they go without, that void is filled with counterfeits, and we all know what some of them are. Unfortunately, the trend of most of this century has been to downplay parenthood as meaningful work for adults. The strong patriarchal father is frowned on by much of society today, to the point that he is almost an endangered species. When I say strong father, I don't mean a grumbling old grizzly who growls at his wife and kids. I mean a man who is strong enough to cultivate self-control and wise enough to realize that the truly strong show their strength by being gentle.

This kind of man will do what husbands and fathers have always done. He will protect his wife and children from the dangers lurking outside and sometimes inside his home. In times past these dangers came from enemies, wild animals, or the forces of nature. Today the dangers are more subtle but no less deadly. Immorality, drug abuse, disrespect for laws and values—these and other poisons can ruin a child's life and canker his soul, and any father worthy of the name will give his last ounce of strength to help his wife and children survive their attacks.

Good fathers do make a difference. Judith S. Brook, an associate professor of psychiatry at Mount Sinai School of Medicine, reported on a study by the National Institute of Drug Abuse. She said, "Fathers who are warm, affectionate, psychologically well-adjusted tend to have both sons and

daughters who are . . . not irresponsible or rebellious."
(*Deseret News*, January 24, 1983, p. A-2.)

What does it take to be a good father? It takes a lot, but
no more than what every man can give if he will. Again
quoting Dr. Daniel Brown, "Actually the things that a baby
needs most cost very little in terms of dollars and cents. He
has never heard of the Joneses. He is unconcerned about
whether you have a million dollars or just enough to pay for
his arrival. He does not care whether you have a nice car or
none at all. He can be as happy in a one-room apartment as
in a ten-room house surrounded with landscaped garden-
ing. What he wants is love, warmth, and acceptance for
himself, . . . strong arms to hold him and make him feel
safe, smiles and cheerfulness, serenity and a sense of order,
someone to come to him when he cries out of his sense of
newness and strangeness. He wants you to not be too busy to
play with him or too serious to enjoy him. He wants you to
stir his awakening mind to a joy and interest in the world
around him. . . . —He wants and needs emotional security." (Brown, p. 706.)

Every man who has a child holds the awesome responsibility of guiding, teaching, and encouraging another
human being who, like himself, is eternal. It is in this that he
draws nearest to the work of God.

33

The Disappearance
of Childhood

Neil Postman has written an intriguing and frightening book called *The Disappearance of Childhood* (New York: Delacorte Press, 1982). It is based on a rather novel idea that childhood is a social invention that was born in the Renaissance and that today is in its death throes. What he basically says is that once there were no children, and soon there will be no children again—only pseudoadults in small bodies.

Consider some of his evidence. In America today, some of the highest paid models are twelve- and thirteen-year-old girls who are seductively, sometimes even pornographically, presented to the public. Between 1950 and 1980, the rate of serious crime committed by those younger than fifteen increased 110 times, or 11,000 percent. With this staggering increase in the number of crimes committed has come an increase in the severity of crimes until more and more children are being tried as adults for adult crimes.

Within the past decade or so, the children's clothing industry has undergone such rapid change that children's clothing has all but disappeared. In the eighteenth century it was put forth by Erasmus and well accepted by the population in general that adults and children required different forms of dress. That is not the case today.

Children's games are meeting the same end. As Neil Postman says, "Who has seen anyone over the age of nine playing Jacks, Johnny on the Pony, Blindman's Buff, or ball-bounding rhymes?" Today children play sports organized and supervised by adults, complete with umpires, uniforms, and spectators.

Those who may doubt the disappearance of children, says Postman, need only to look at television for evidence. Children appear there, all right, but in adult roles. They are pitchmen for products including sausages, real estate, toothpaste, and detergent. In the situational comedies they are wise-cracking smart alecks, and in the movies they have shifted from the charming innocence of a Shirley Temple to smaller versions of adults with language, behavior, and interests suitable to adults. Children's literature is following a similar track with language and themes that used to be reserved for adults.

Such observations on the disappearance of childhood could continue to mount, but proving that point is not what Postman tries to do in his book. Indeed, he says, "Wherever I have gone to speak, or whenever I have written, on the subject of the disappearance of childhood, audiences and readers have not only refrained from disputing the point but have eagerly provided me with evidence of it from their own experience. The observation that the dividing line between childhood and adulthood is rapidly eroding is common enough among those who are paying attention, and is even suspected by those who are not. What isn't so well understood is where childhood comes from in the first place and, still less, why it should be disappearing."

Postman says that the Greeks and Romans had some social idea of childhood. Though the Greeks had no legal or moral restraints against infanticide and never pictured children in their great pieces of art, they did establish schools for boys. The Romans borrowed the Greek notion of school and even developed an awareness of childhood as a special time that surpassed the Greek idea. Roman art, for instance, revealed an extraordinary sense of the young and growing child. This is not to suppose, however, that either the Greeks or the Romans had an idea of childhood parallel to the modern one. Indeed, methods of disciplining children during that time would be considered cruel by us. "The evidence which I have collected on methods of disciplining children," noted Lloyd DeMause, "leads me to believe that a very large percentage of the children prior to the eighteenth century were what would today be termed battered children." DeMause conjectures that a "hundred generations of mothers" impassively watched their infants and children suffer from one source of discomfort or another because the mothers lacked the psychic mechanisms necessary to empathize with children.

At any rate, with the fall of Rome and the cloud over civilization known as the Middle Ages, society lost any sense of childhood. Part of this was certainly because society lost the values of literacy and education. Adults and children alike lived in an oral world. There was no body of knowledge that adults had access to that children did not. Children shared with adults the same games, the same toys, the same fairy stories. They were not shielded in any way from the mysteries, contradictions, violence, and tragedy of life. They were not shielded from any particular kinds of language or behavior. Infancy ended at age of seven and adulthood began immediately. There was no intervening stage of development, and indeed there seemed to be no need for it.

Historian Barbara Tuchman sums it up this way: "Of all the characteristics in which the medieval age differs from the modern, none is so striking as the comparative absence of interest in children."

It was the printing press that changed all that and gave birth finally to childhood. The reason is that from this time onward, children had to become adults by gaining a specialized skill, namely reading. Society began to view children as separate from adults, and once that was accomplished, they began to be viewed as having different needs and different natures as well. What all of this led to was a remarkable change in the social status of the young. Children came to be seen not as miniature adults, but as unformed adults who deserved some sort of special protection and training. Schools were developed with sequential courses. Special books for children began to be printed. The family took on a new and enhanced role as parents assumed new responsibilities as guardians, protectors, nurturers, and arbiters of taste. Adults were able to control the environment of children and set strict standards for entry into adulthood, such as self-control and the ability to delay gratification. In this way, interestingly enough, the birth of childhood brought about the birth of adulthood as well.

But what the printing press seemed to bring about, another form of communication is busy undoing today. Neil Postman says that television is obliterating childhood. The reason is that it is moving us back into a society where there is little distinction between adults and children. Television is a total disclosure medium; it tells all and children are once again exposed, as they were in the Middle Ages, to the mysteries, contradiction, violence, and tragedy of adulthood life. They are shielded and protected from little, and this is happening as the means of learning is shifting from the abstract, sequential world of print to the easy-access world of the picture tube. The result is a blur between what were once the separate worlds of adult and children, and both groups are diminished by it. In fact, it is not too much to suppose that our whole society will be undermined by this new cultural tendency to undo children.

What can be done by it? After all, very few of us would come out against childhood if we could help it. Postman offers no answers for society as a whole, but he does give some ideas for individuals who are willing to resist the trend. He says, "Resistance entails conceiving of parenting as an act of rebellion against American culture. For example, for parents merely to remain married is itself an act of disobedience and an insult to the spirit of a throwaway culture in which continuity has little value. It is also at least ninety percent un-American to remain in close proximity to one's extended family so that children can experience, daily, the meaning of kinship and the value of deference and responsibility to elders. Similarly, to insist that one's children learn the discipline of delayed gratification . . . or self-restraint in manners, language and style is to place oneself in opposition to almost every social trend. . . . But most rebellious of all is the attempt to control the media's access to one's children. There are, in fact, two ways to do this. The first is to limit the amount of exposure children have to media. The second is to monitor carefully what they are exposed to."

Postman concludes that these ideas are difficult and in fact defying the very culture in which we live. But if we care about our children having a childhood, they are worth it.

34

What We Owe
Our Children

A few weeks ago I was talking to a family counselor about a subject that is never too far from any parent's mind—the question of what we can do to help our children. I expected from his background a long list of practical, helpful hints and do's and don'ts about how to ease my children's journey through life and help them reach their full potential. I guess I wasn't quite ready for his response.

He said, "When I was young, I wanted to be a baseball player, and I wanted to be a writer, and I even wanted to be a dance instructor. But I never got much support from my parents, particularly my father. I know now that he was busy on the farm, and times were tough, and it was the Depression, and a lot of other reasons. But when you're young, you don't see those things. I saw only the things I could have been if he had given me the chance."

My friend paused long and thought way back. Then he added, "I wasted an embarrassing amount of time thinking those thoughts for a good part of my life. Finally it came to me that, in this great land of opportunity, you can do pretty much what you want to do. It was not my father's fault that I did not achieve some of the things I said I wanted. But he was the easiest scapegoat for my own lack of effort and desire."

He continued, "I've told my children, 'If you want to be something, go out and be it, and I'll back you all I can, but don't blame me if you don't fulfill your dreams.'" Then he smiled. "Does that sound harsh, unfeeling? Well, all I know is that one of our children has excelled on the trumpet. Another one wanted to be a bicycle racer. I told him fine, I'd help him. I guess he had some talent. The next thing I knew he was in the state finals and went on to take second place in the Western Regionals. My wife and our family were there to cheer him on whenever we could, but I sure didn't pedal his bicycle."

Interesting observations, I thought. They reminded me of the words of one of America's most popular advice givers, Ann Landers. She wrote, "What do parents owe their children? It is easier to start with what you do not owe them. You do not owe them every minute of your day or every ounce of your energy. Nor do you owe them round-the-clock chauffeur service, horseback-riding lessons, singing lessons, summer camp, ski outfits and ten-speed bikes, a motorcycle or a car when they turn 16, or a trip to Europe when they graduate.

"I take the firm position that parents do not owe their children a college education. By all means send them to college if you can afford it, but don't feel guilty if you can't. If they really want to go, they'll find a way. . . .

"After children marry, you do not owe them a down payment on a home or money for furniture. Nor do you have an obligation to baby-sit with their kids or take over when they go on vacation. If you want to do any of these things, it should be considered an act of generosity, not an obligation.

"Parents do not owe their progeny an inheritance, no matter how much money they have." She concludes, "One of the surest ways to produce loafers and freeloaders is to let children know that their future is assured." (*Family Circle,* November 15, 1977, pp. 85-86.)

I seem to remember the instructions of an old king of England to the nurses caring for his son. He told them that this was the heir to the throne, and at no time was he to be denied anything he wanted. The nurses tried faithfully to fulfill that command, and the baby they brought up became a monstrous slave to his own appetites and passions. He sacrificed his subjects in wars to feed his inflated ego. He exiled one wife and murdered two others. He stirred up strife and hatred in his own family, and it spread through the kingdom and brought on England's civil war. Thus was the career of King Henry the Eighth, who grew up believing somebody owed him everything.

I do not want to add to some guilt complex that seems to have already gotten us into enough difficulties, but I think it is fair to say that a big part of the problem is that we, as parents, have not given our children too much, but too little of the really important things. Too little time, too little concern, too little attention when it really counted. A successful father told me once, "The willow whistle you make with your child at age six is worth much more than the car you might give him at sixteen."

Willow whistles, walks in the woods, time to listen to them as they grow—these are priceless treasures we have forgotten to share.

Years ago, a schoolteacher invited fathers in to hear essays from their children. The fathers came that night in overalls and blue serge suits, driving four hundred dollar cars and forty thousand dollar cars—men from all walks of life. They heard the children read their essays about how they felt about their dads. "I like my dad because he talks to me." "I like my dad because he took me fishing." "I like my dad because he plays ball with me." Not one essayist wrote, "I like my dad because he sits on the stock exchange," "I like

my dad because he's chairman of the board," or "I like
him because he buys me everything I want." No, it was the
greater treasures that these children appreciated.

Yes, indeed, we owe our children a lot, but we do not
owe them the things they can gain themselves. To quote
again from Ann Landers, "One of the chief obligations parents have is to give their children a sense of personal worth.
Self-esteem is the cornerstone for good mental health. A
youngster who is continually criticized and 'put down,'
made to feel stupid and inept, . . . will become so unsure, so
terrified of failing that he or she won't try at all.

"The child who is repeatedly called 'bad' or 'naughty' or
'no good' will behave in a way that justifies the parents' description. Children have an uncanny way of living up—or
down—to what is expected of them.

"Of course, they should be corrected and set straight—
this is the way children learn—but criticism should be heavily outweighed by praise."

She goes on to counsel parents that if you can't say it,
show it—a smile, a touch. These are powerful com-
municators with which we can encourage our children.

By all means, we should give our children firm, strong
guidelines. Despite what they may say, it is terrifying for a
growing child to live in a world where there are no reassur-
ing fences to push against.

We should help our children feel good about the marvelous creation that is the body, help them to respect it and
never defile it with drugs, or immorality, or debilitating
habits. A sense of values is priceless to a child, and we, as
parents, owe this to them. It has been truthfully said that
values are not taught so much as they are caught.

And we should give our children a solid religious foundation on which to build their lives. If our own religious
faith needs more support, there are tried and true ways to

make it solid for sure. For our own sake and the sake of our children, we must bring the Lord into our lives.

May we pay those loving obligations every day to those we love so much, so that they, in turn, may grow up strong and free, independent and loving, and pass these gifts on to their children and to their children's children.

35

Peer Pressure vs. Family Pressure

One of the great rights guaranteed by the United States Constitution is the right to be tried by a jury of one's peers. This is to safeguard us against tyranny from unjust judges. But what about the tyranny of our peers, particularly among our young people? I'm not talking about judgments and verdicts in a courtroom. Rather, I am talking about judgments of how we shall govern the actions of our everyday lives.

Recently a national organization conducted a survey to find out whom young people look to for example and direction. They found that some disquieting changes had occurred over the past twenty years. In 1960, parents were the primary source of guidance for young people, followed by teachers, and then friends and peers. By 1980, these advisers had reshuffled significantly. At the top of the totem pole, the group ranking number one was the peer group.

Now I have nothing against friends and peers. They are indispensable, invaluable, priceless to a person growing up. What would we do without friends to bounce our ideas off, share our joys and disappointments, and generally learn together with as we grow? But that is just the point. Your peers and mine are learning right along with us. They have no claim to greater wisdom for having lived longer and experienced more. That is why they are our peers. They may be struggling for survival emotionally, physically, intellectually, and spiritually just as we are. And when one is bouncing from rock to rock in the turbulent torrents of the teens, he has a difficult time setting anchor on another person who is fighting the same white water. He needs someone more stable, more sure, more solid, more experienced; someone who cares deeply about him.

Fortunately, the Lord has set up this world to provide each of us with such a someone—actually two "someones"—our parents. These are people who have come into this world just a few years ahead of us. They are close enough so they can still vividly remember how tough it is to grow up, but distant enough from us to give us a little perspective, a little longer-range view. Parents have been blessed with something else from heaven, a natural love for their offspring that cannot be matched by any peer group, PTA, scout troop, and certainly not any street gang. Their lives are wrapped around and intertwined with ours in a way that no other relationship in this world will ever be. Long after we have ceased to be a student, a soldier, a senator, a surgeon, or whatever, we will still be a son or a daughter to those who gave us birth. That is an eternal relationship, and one which you and I should treasure, support, build, and rely on all the days of our lives.

In the 1960s, the battle cry of the counterculture was "Never trust anybody older than thirty." One can't help but wonder how today's thirty-five- and forty-year-olds who rallied to that cry feel about that advice now. Perhaps they look to the present young generation in sadness and wish they would take sound advice and save themselves a repetition of the same mistakes. Perhaps they would like to reach back and help the younger generation along. But apparently the seeds sown during that decade have borne quiet fruit in the hearts of many young people. The so-called generation gap still yawns between too many parents and children today.

What is the cause of this, and what can be done about it? Let's look at the other side of this question. I have come down pretty hard and heavily on young people who prefer the counsel and example of their peers over their elders, and particularly their parents. This is a serious shortcoming, and one I would not belittle, but there is another side to this inoperative equation. That is, what kind of example, counsel, and caring are young people getting from parents and other adult advisers?

Though I have painted a glowing picture of a loving, caring, and wise mother and father looking solicitously to the security of their sons and daughters, no one knows better than the youth that this is not always the case. "Latchkey kids" come home after school to find the key under the mat, the house quiet and empty. They have nothing but an amiable TV set in the living room or wandering friends in the street to spend their time with. They can't feel too well cared for. We have a soaring divorce rate, resulting in single-parent households with one person given the awesome burden of trying to provide for as well as nurture the family circle. We are faced with an appalling rate of abortions. Youth and children cannot see such statistics and not think at least momentarily, "There but for fortunate timing and convenient circumstances go I." Birth is made less sacred and children less secure by such statistics.

I would not belittle the economic and social pressures on people in our time. They are very real. I only ask us to weigh them in the balance and compare them to the costs of losing the trusting eyes of our children upon us. If we force them to turn to teachers, television, or peer groups as substitutes for the natural examples, counselors, and loving leaders they have a right to in this world, we will reap a sorrowful reward and our children will wander through life's wilderness without proper guides.

I do not point the finger of accusation at youth, adults, parents, or children, but I plead with young people to reach out and forgive us of the older generation for our transgressions both of ignoring and being ignorant to their needs. I plead with parents, in the words of David O. McKay, to "let love abound. Though you fall short in some material matters, study and work and pray to hold your children's love." (*Improvement Era*, April 1962, p. 252.) And I plead for our society not to put undue pressures and impossible obstacles in the paths of parents, children, and families, but to support with every means possible that sacred institution which has been and will continue to be the salvation of society: the family.

36

Making People Change

Of all the false assumptions that plague us, the worst may be that we could be happy if we could just make someone else change. Many of us pick on our spouses. We think, "If he were only more understanding, more thoughtful, less sloppy, then I could be happy." "If she could only control her temper, watch her weight, then I could be happy."

If we don't have a list of changes for our partners, then we often look to our children. We are made miserable by their bad grades or sharp tongues, and have grand plans to remake them to suit us.

Some of us look to our colleagues at work. If they would only change, how happy we could be. If they would be more generous, less territorial, then life could be almost perfect.

And on it goes. We have grand plans to revise those whom we know, and we're sure life would be better when they change. But there are some things we ought to know before we start trying to change someone else.

First, people don't change significantly because we force them to. Every parent of every child finally discovers this. "If you don't have this room cleaned in one hour, you can't go with us on the picnic," says the parent. One hour later, he comes into the sloppy room and says, "All right, you can't go on the picnic; and if you don't have your room cleaned by tomorrow, you're grounded for a week." The next day, he comes into a sloppy room and says, "If you don't have this room cleaned by tonight, you're grounded for a month, and you can't watch TV." The next day, that same parent comes into the sloppy room and finally shouts, "You're grounded for life!" If the parent really could enforce such a verdict, the child would probably spend most of that life sitting in his sloppy room.

People are the agents of their own change. We can inspire our children and encourage them. As parents, we can lay down some strict rules, and we should, hoping that good behavior will grow line upon line until it is habitual. But we really cannot force people to change. People change permanently only when *they* decide to. It is when we think that we can force them, conform them to our idea of what they ought to be, that relationships are ruptured.

Next, people don't change significantly because we show disgust or anger for their current behavior. They may respond to our desire for them to change temporarily to overcome the punishment of our anger, but it usually doesn't last.

I know of one father who was trying to teach his son to ride a two-wheeled bicycle. The little boy was clearly afraid and balked at all the instructions. The father tried to shame him into learning, saying that all the other kids his age could do it, and why couldn't he? The boy still resisted. Finally the father walked away in disgust, leaving the little boy crying beside his bicycle, feeling ashamed of himself but no less willing to learn. When the father was asked why he handled the situation that way, he replied, "I couldn't think of any other way to make him change." What the onlooker could have pointed out is that the way he thought of didn't work either.

Finally, people don't change merely because we think they ought to. People do what they do for good reasons, even if those reasons aren't readily apparent to us. They are responding to their own maps of reality, which don't change merely by having someone else suggest different behavior.

One couple who were engaged to be married found that out the hard way. They were riding in a car up in the mountains in the early spring, trying to follow a back road into the bride-to-be's cabin. Of course, there were still mounds of snow, and the road was very muddy. When the going began to get rough, she wanted to turn around and go back. Her fiancé wanted to go forward until they got stuck to see just how far they could make it. As they talked, their points of view seemed irreconcilable, and she started to think how reckless he was and wished he could be different. He considered her overly cautious and wished she could have been a little more daring.

Instead of fighting about their different approaches, however, they decided to discuss them. She was prudent because her family was. Who could think it would be fun to be stuck? He thought of it as merely adventure because he had been brought up with a derring-do attitude. Neither one was likely to change merely because the other wanted him or her to. They finally compromised without anger. "He went alone," she said with a laugh, "and got stuck."

People face life and each event in it with very different expectations. These expectations are grounded in their personalities, their experience, their triumphs, and their disappointments. The behavior these expectations elicit is not likely to change just because we want it to.

So, with all these unworkable solutions for changing people, what are we to do about the people in our lives we'd like to change? Probably we ought to approach the subject with much more humility than we usually do. As La Rochefoucauld said, "It is easier to be wise for others than for ourselves."

The only person we can change with absolute assurance that our program will work is ourself. Each of us is in-complete. Each of us is weak. Each of us is thoughtless in some ways, lacking in others. It is here that we need to con-centrate our efforts. We each need to change ourself. Our Lord Jesus Christ gave us that advice nearly two thousand years ago: "Why beholdest thou the mote that is in thy brother's eye, but considerest not the beam that is in thine own eye?" (Matthew 7:3.)

The problem, of course, is that the ways our friends and families need to change are so obvious to us, and our own faults are so obscure. In fact, often we fall into the trap described by La Rochefoucauld: "We confess our little faults only to persuade others that we have no great ones."

Let us be aware of our faults—not enough to be over-come by them or overwhelmed by how far we need to go, but enough that we tackle change with some gusto. It is, after all, the person we see in the glass that we have to live with the most.

When we are tempted to force, shame, or prod others around us to change, let us love them instead. Let us accept them where they are and confirm their worth in their own eyes by letting them know they have worth in ours. It is only in such an atmosphere of acceptance and love that others can change anyway. Nothing else but love can ever perma-nently motivate. It is the royal law.

Section 4

HEROES AND ROLE MODELS

37

Everyday Heroes

This is a story that most of us can identify with in a measure. We have seen or heard some variation on it at some time in our lives. I got the story from Kathleen Pulsipher, and it comes from her high school days.

In Kathleen's school was a girl who had a broad, rather plain face and a wide smile. Often that smile was strained at the corners and fixed determinedly on her mouth as she tried to clump along through life and through the halls of that high school on a twisted leg. She hobbled more on the side of her ankle than on her foot. This alone would test the limits of one's smile, but in addition, she had to carry the burden of thoughtless classmate comedians who occasionally enjoyed imitating her to get a cheap laugh at her expense.

The smile of the young woman endured. But one day, in one of those minor incidents that can turn into a major tragedy in a person's life, her shoe fell off as she was hobbling down the hall. As she was struggling to put it back on and not lose her balance, one of the school pranksters kicked the shoe and sent it spinning down the hall. Immediately, in that unexplainable stupidity that turns normal people into a mob, all the kids in the hall took up the game and began to jeer and make fun of the young woman with the twisted leg.

Not even her determination could hold up against such heavy pressure. That solid smile that had endured so much began to droop as the tears welled up in her eyes.

Oh, why do we in the crowd so seldom see those who are suffering outside our circle and need a gentle hand to bring them in? The crowd did not see. Like a pack of jackals, they baited her to see what she would do next.

But then, pushing through the crowd came the broad shoulders of one of the finest athletes in the school. His eyes were cold steel boring through the crowd, and his jaw was set solid. He was one of the most popular young men in that school, but he was much more than popular. He was a man in the noblest sense of the term. He retrieved the worn corrective shoe and brought it back to the crippled girl. He did not say anything, but his eyes looking into hers said, "I am sorry." And her shy eyes said, "I am grateful."

An ashamed rabble melted into the high school corridors and returned to their natural state as students. A heroic act had pulled them back to sanity and shown them how human beings behave toward one another.

Saving a beautiful damsel in distress is a chivalrous deed, but helping a crippled child of our Father in heaven is a mark of truly noble character. "Inasmuch as ye have done it unto one of the least of these my brethren, ye have done it unto me." (Matthew 25:40.) So spoke the Christ, the noblest hero in history.

Though he was the greatest of all, Jesus generally chose to be among the humble people. He did not wear the laurel crown of victory. He chaired no great committees, ruled no nation, commanded no armies. Eventually he gave his life in the most degrading and shameful form of execution that demented men could devise. "Inasmuch as ye have done it unto the least of these my brethren," he instructed us. Who are the least of those among us whom the Lord would claim as his brethren, and how shall we serve them?

I know a family with two children of their own and eight more they have gathered from orphanages and refugee camps around the world. Because of them, children left homeless by war and tragedy now have a second shot at survival in this world. My friends, the parents of these little people, are providing for the least of the Lord's children.

I know a woman with a sweet, soothing voice who spends a good part of her time in hospitals and homes for the aged. There she sings to those tired and worthy hearts a bit of comfort in the last years they will spend in this life. Our society has relegated the venerable old to a cast-off role. They seem to be the least important to many people—but they are not so to my friend with the beautiful voice.

Another family I know has sort of adopted a young inmate at the state prison. Frequently they visit him and hold a family home evening together. Prison bars make an unusual background for games, songs, and family stories, but for them it is a joyful experience because they are doing it to benefit one who might be considered among the least valuable in our society.

There is a scoutmaster in our city who is one of the most successful leaders of young men I have ever seen, yet his boys have never won a competition against other troops. But they have won contests in the toughest league in the world, the competition with themselves. If they can cook an edible meal, hike up a hill, sometimes even tie their own scout bandelo, that to them is a great victory, because they are mentally handicapped. To most people they are among the least important among us. But to their scoutmaster they are young men of potential and pride. And when he sees them conquer some small hill that to them is Mount Everest, his eyes sparkle just about as much as theirs do. They love him, and so does the Lord.

"Inasmuch as ye have done it unto the least of these my brethren, ye have done it unto me." Why does the Lord direct our attention so strongly to the disadvantaged among us? Partly for their sakes, but also for ours. We need to know that we are doing good for the right reasons. It is easy to help those who are in a position to return the favor. It is difficult to know how pure our motives are when a reward is dangling too obviously at the end of our labors. But to befriend the friendless, to share with those who can never repay us, to give love to the unloveable—these and other acts begin to develop within us a godly character and a deep joy that is obtainable in no other way.

I pray that we may walk with a helping hand and a compassionate heart as we go through this world, that we may see in the face of every needy person the reflected suffering of our Lord. Alexander Pope wrote two hundred fifty years ago,

> *Teach me to feel another's woe,*
> *To hide the fault I see;*
> *That mercy I to others show,*
> *That mercy show to me.*

Surely the Lord has shown great mercy to each of us, and all that he asks in return is that we serve one another and ease the burdens and pain of his children in this world.

38

Appreciation—Starting Now

Someone once said that if the stars came out only once a century, the whole world would turn out to see them. Television networks would vie for coverage. The scientific community would prepare years in advance. The headlines would be full of nothing else, and all of us would stare at the sky that night with wonder in our hearts.

But, of course, the stars come out every night, so we hardly see them.

That is the way life is. Sometimes we only appreciate what we have done without. Scarcity teaches us appreciation. We see things clearly only in their absence. There is no drink of water so cool and quenching as the one following a desert walk with an empty canteen. Few can see the joys of children more poignantly than the childless couple. The sun never shines so brightly as at the end of a long siege of storms.

I heard one man say that the best restaurant at which he had ever eaten was the back of a tank on his way into Paris as the war was ending in Europe. The food was only K rations, but he says that no gourmet offering has ever tasted so good.

It is ironic that plenty does not teach us gratitude as well as privation. We learn happiness by experiencing sorrow. We value security when we have known insecurity. We rejoice in light because we have known the darkness. And maybe that is why older people with their bundle of experiences find more to be thankful for at Thanksgiving than children who have yet to understand.

Appreciation is a lesson that Diane Ellingson learned. She was a member of the University of Utah women's gymnastics team, and in 1981 she placed second on the uneven bars at the national collegiate championships. Her team won their first championship that year, and she stood proudly with them in the middle of the floor while the crowd roared their approval in a standing ovation. Little did she know that she would be in the same place the next year while the crowd cheered for the Utes' second championship. This time the ovation was even bigger, and she was in a wheelchair—a spectator instead of a participant. The reason was that in December 1981, she fell from a balancing horse in Miami while preparing for a thirteen-week professional gymnastics tour, and severed the spinal cord between her sixth and seventh vertebrae, paralyzing her from the chest down.

At first, in her Florida hospital room, Diane did not realize the permanence of her injuries. "Things were great in Florida," she says. "I was still happy, and everyone was so nice. I had no idea it would last very long. I was sure I would be out of the hospital and competing again within a month." (*Deseret News*, July 24, 1983.)

That was not to be. She was transferred to the University of Utah Medical Center, where her head was put in traction for forty days. At first, she kept up her happy face for the rush of visitors; she didn't want anyone to think she was miserable. But finally depression hit. She said, "The visitors slacked off, and it was becoming so frustrating in traction. I was a prisoner, not only in the hospital, but within my own body."

Reporters wanted to interview her, but she kept them away. She knew she wasn't ready. As she looked at the lifeless legs, the hands crippled from the knuckles, there were some things she had to face. She wasn't going to get better. She would never again compete in a gymnastics meet, though she had trained six hours a day, six days a week for that. Her life, which had been founded on disciplined, physical activity, would be a struggle in just moving from one place to another. Could she take it? Was that competitive spirit which had refreshed and motivated her life as a gymnast alive and well enough to still make her a winner at life's challenges?

Diane said, "I decided the direction of my life hadn't changed. It was just slowed down a bit. I had decided after my senior year that my gymnastics career was over, and it was time to move on to something else. When I was a gymnast, I wanted to be the best. . . . I wanted to be famous. Now I don't want to be famous, but I want to be the best I can be within myself. I want to be the best teacher. I want to get married some day and be the best wife and the best mother I can be."

It is because of that attitude that she wheeled out on the floor after her team had won the 1982 national collegiate championships. That night the crowd cheered when they saw her. It was an outpouring of love and admiration, not just for her gymnastic ability, but for a far greater achievement—the unquenchable spirit of a human soul who fights on bravely against grim odds.

Still, perhaps the most compelling part of Diane's story is that she continues to go forward without collapsing into a heap of self-pity. In fact, far from it. Her accident has given her life a depth of appreciation most of us lack.

"I am a deeper person now," she said. "I am a person who understands a lot more about happiness, because I have felt pain. I can appreciate more the experiences I had as a gymnast, because now I see the other side." She wants to write a book someday about her experiences, but she says that she's not ready to do that yet: "I'm not satisfied with the ending."

So all of us are about writing our life's story. And to a great extent, whether it is a rich story or a meager one will depend on our ability to appreciate what is right before us. The poorest souls in the world are those who, having everything, are always grasping for more. They think that another house, another job, another vacation, or another possession will heal the ache. They are deluding themselves.

Those who are most joyous are those who can make a bouquet of the flowers right at hand. Why do we always want something else when we have yet to discover and revel in what we already have? It is human nature to appreciate something only after we've lost it. Let us resolve to do better and to find joy in what is already ours. Those among us who do so are the happy ones like Diane Ellingson. The rest of us waste a lifetime, waiting for something more.

39

Success in All Seasons

In a third grade room, the teacher announced to the class, "Peter is both stupid and lazy." Now, that kind of inspiring evaluation might be the death knell of academic interest for most eight-year-olds, but somehow Peter survived it, and today the formerly so-called stupid and lazy Peter is one of America's leading authorities on work and production. His many books and innumerable lectures are the source of wisdom for business leaders throughout the world. His name: Peter Drucker.

Such surprising success stories are not just a phenomenon of our day, of course. More than a century ago a dull and sickly little boy named Waldo trudged to the school he hated. His mother described him as unimaginative and held no great hopes for him. He fulfilled her expectations by being poor in math and possessing a singularly weak memory for Greek conjugations. But somewhere, somehow, his intellect caught fire. He began to devour books and to force-feed his mind with great thoughts. He was up at five every morning to write his own thoughts in what he called his "idea savings bank." The world has drawn heavily on that bank since his time—grateful for the little dull schoolboy who would one day be called the wisest American, Ralph Waldo Emerson.

And, speaking of books, words, and language, there was another slow student who just couldn't seem to get the hang of the King's English. Fortunately a patient teacher helped him get rolling, or there might not be any king's England today. Who else could have thundered these immortal words across the channel at the Nazi war machine: "We shall not flag or fail. We shall go on to the end. We shall fight in France, we shall fight on the seas and oceans, we shall fight with growing confidence and growing strength in the air, we shall defend our island, whatever the cost may be, we shall fight on the beaches, we shall fight on the landing grounds, we shall fight in the fields and in the streets, we shall fight in the hills; we shall never surrender. . . .

"Let us therefore brace ourselves to our duties, and so bear ourselves that, if the British Empire and its Commonwealth last for a thousand years, men will still say: 'This was their finest hour.'"

I do believe Sir Winston Churchill did get the hang of the language. I should add, though, that he never did come to feel very comfortable with numbers. Cramming his hardest, he still took three times to pass the army entrance exams. Probably it's just as well. If he had been a math whiz, he might have figured out England's chances of surviving the war and surrendered.

There was another man, however, who was quick with figures but pathetically slow with everything else. Not only that, but he had a bad attitude—so bad that he was asked to leave high school because he was having a negative effect on other students. He tried to enter a technical university but flunked the entrance exam, so he went back to a confining high school to try again. He then went on to graduate from high school and college. After that, he took a menial job in a patent office, and in his spare time he rearranged our universe. This high school dropout was Albert Einstein.

These stories might be used for consolation when

report-card time comes around. But the real point behind them is that each of us is gifted in some things, perhaps not so talented in others. And we all have our own biological clock of development. Some of us are late bloomers and some unfold into more flashy flowers, but we all have the potential for greatness within us.

So don't be discouraged if you didn't graduate from grade school at the top of your class. You're in pretty good company. For every child prodigy, you can find an elderly wonder in history. For every Mozart concertizing at the age of three, you can find an Aristotle who didn't flower until the age when many people are almost ready to retire. For every Alexander the Great who conquered his known world while still in his twenties, you can find an Abraham Lincoln who hardly won an election until he was fifty—but then held the nation together almost singlehandedly.

It is not when or where or even how we make our contribution. The only important thing is that we contribute. No matter where we find ourselves on the scale of years in school or years in life, our best years can still be in front of us. As the old saying goes, this is the first day of the rest of our life.

I talked with a friend once who wanted to go to college, but he had a job and a family. He said, "It would take me ten years. By the time I got out I would be thirty-five years old." I said, "Well, if you don't go to school, how old will you be in ten years?"

The best years of our lives are whenever we choose to make them. I believe it was Leo Durocher, the successful and feisty manager of the old Brooklyn Dodgers, who was once asked, "In your long career in baseball, what was your greatest moment?" Durocher snapped back as only he could, "I haven't had it yet."

Neither have you had your greatest moment yet, and neither have I. So let us look forward to every sunrise and to what that day may bring. Let us give thanks to God for the life he has given us, for the days that lie before us, and for the opportunities to serve others and thereby serve him, and in that service to find our best selves. As Jesus said, "Whosoever shall lose his life for my sake and the gospel's, the same shall save it." (Mark 8:35.) That is true both in this life and in the endless life that awaits us when we finish our work here.

40

What It Means to Win

In the summer of 1984, I was primed and ready to cheer the champions in Los Angeles. When Olympic athletes do their superb best, they serve an admirable and needed function in our world. They give even the most sedentary among us a shot of motivation and a desire to raise our own goals. It is inspirational to see the combination of talent and training that makes a champion.

What is a champion? In the Olympics of 1936 held in Berlin, Germany, there were two great champions, in my mind. The first and most famous was Jesse Owens, the American all-around track man who brought home four gold medals from those games. There was also another champion that day—a man whose name you probably don't know. He didn't take home the gold medal; he won the second place silver, but he won something much more valuable. His name was Luz Long.

In the preliminary trials in the long jump, Long, a German, saw his fellow athlete from America disqualified twice. He suggested to Jesse Owens that he jump back several inches from the line. Owens followed his advice, qualified, and went on to win the long jump and set a new world's record. In those qualifying jumps, it would have been easy for Luz Long to quietly turn his head and let Jesse

Owens be disqualified. But Long was not just physically a champion. He was an Olympian in heart and character. For him it was more important that the best man win than that he himself win. But there is more to the story.

Jesse Owens was a black man. It flew in the face of Hitler's pernicious doctrines of racial superiority that a so-called inferior race could beat his blond and blue-eyed Aryans. The Führer refused to recognize or acknowledge a black champion. But there were Germans made of finer stuff than their Führer; and, as Jesse Owens walked back along the track in front of the stadium, he was accompanied very obviously by Germany's finest long jumper, Luz Long. As they stood to acknowledge the accolades of the crowd, Long deliberately put his arms around his fellow athlete and embraced him. Jesse Owens later recalled that as "an act of special grace and special courtesy to a fellow athlete." (Cleveland Amory, "Good Guys, Bad Guys, *Parade*, March 20, 1983.) I would call it the mark of a real champion.

The physical accomplishments we cheer about are not really all that phenomenal. Other animals can far outdistance us in running, jumping, and strength. But when the human spirit soars, that is the most breathtaking act in all creation. When a human heart rises above its selfishness and sets a record in integrity, compassion, fair play, honesty, and the other real contests of life, nothing on earth can match it.

It's good to know that such acts still happen. Some time ago a professional tennis player named Eliot Teltscher won his match, but in his final volley, he touched the net with his racket, disqualifying his championship point. No one saw it, not even the judges, but Teltscher felt the tick of the net on his racket. He only had to keep silent to claim the contest. To speak up would cost him the match, but it would gain him the satisfaction of being a competitor in the truest sense. He chose to speak.

Today we commonly excuse all kinds of petulant behavior in and out of the game with the feeble excuse that he or she is a real competitor who loves to win above all. Let me tell you about a real competitor.

Many years ago at Princeton a young man named Hoby Baker played the rough-and-tumble iron-man's game they called football in those days. The only sport more physical was hockey, and he also played that. It is recorded that, in the course of one hockey melee, the official called a foul. Hoby Baker protested. Now this is certainly not an unusual scene for us today. We see disputed calls, rhubarbs, and an occasional roundhouse in hockey and other sports regularly. But Baker's dispute was different. He was arguing for his opposition. He said, "They were not going after me, sir, they were playing the puck. If you charge them with a foul, they might well lose the game." It is recorded that the referee shrugged his shoulders, said, "What next," and reversed himself.

Several years later, this great athlete and great competitor was playing against a professional hockey team that used every dirty trick in the book, including banging his head on the ice when he was down. It is also history that, following the game, Baker went to the opposition's dressing room, as was his custom, and thanked them for the game, telling them that he enjoyed it. It is recorded from their own admission that they were ashamed.

Real champions learn that victory over themselves is much more important than victory over an opponent. They know the truth of the biblical wisdom, "He that is slow to anger is better than the mighty; and he that ruleth his spirit than he that taketh a city." (Proverbs 16:32.) Or, we might add, he that taketh a gold medal.

I'm all for winning if we understand what it really means to win. Winning is not racking up a higher score. Winning is attaining a higher character. The contest of life is not on the playing floor, field, or track. It is within the human heart. The score is not added up at some scorer's table. It is tallied in each individual conscience. In the last analysis, none of us is in competition with another. We are all unique. The contest for victory is with one's self.

And the prize is not a laurel wreath such as the ancient Olympians won—a wreath that will fade and dry and crumble. It is not even a gold medal that may withstand the elements for a time, but eventually will disintegrate. The prize is an eternal spirit molded through adherence to eternal truth into the greatest creation in the universe.

May we take this spirit with us as we cheer our favorite athletes and teams, and may we be inspired by their efforts to redouble our own efforts in our own contest—the most important contest we can ever face.

41

Lessons from the Olympics

Twenty-seven centuries ago, several athletes gathered to run a 200-yard footrace. The winner was one Coroebus of Elis. In so doing, he went into the record books as the first Olympic champion we know of. That little footrace has come a long way since that day in Olympia, Greece, and it has produced some interesting champions along the way. In the ancient days, there was Milo of Croton, an undefeated six-time wrestling champion who trained by carrying a calf on his shoulders every day until it had grown into a full-sized bull.

Today's training techniques are a bit more sophisticated, and the events are more diverse; but the purpose of the Olympics is still the same—to discover and display the finest athletes in the world. I get excited about seeing this kind of greatness, not just because it's a thrill to see athletes do their thing so well, but because there are lessons of life to be gained from Olympic contests.

For one thing, Joe Pietro might tell us that size doesn't have much to do with championship performance. Joe was a bantamweight gold-medal weightlifter for America in 1948, and he was only four feet six inches tall. On the other hand, Chris Taylor, a 1972 Olympic wrestler, weighed 420 pounds.

We think of the Olympics as a young person's game, and usually it is. Sonja Henie, the great Norwegian figure skater, was only ten when she first competed. But Artur von Pongracz might tell us, "Don't count out the gray power here." He was seventy-two years young when he competed with the Austrian equestrian team.

Al Oerter might tell us it is the mind and spirit as much as the body that makes a champion. With torn ligaments in his rib cage, Al hobbled out of the hospital in 1964 and painfully stepped into the circle, hoping he could get off just one discus throw. With his body wrapped like a mummy and his side packed in ice, he threw not once, but twice, then three, four, and five of his permitted six tries. He not only won the gold; he also set a new world's record of 200 feet 1½ inches. Pain is often the price of victory.

Another key to success in sports and in life is that you don't quit when the going gets rough. A young swimmer in the Mexico City Olympics of 1968 proved that. He was supposed to dazzle the world, but something went wrong and he came home empty-handed. Instead of giving up, he got back to work training even harder than before. Four years later, Mark Spitz fulfilled his potential and brought home seven gold medals.

Randy Matson might remind us that fame is fleeting. He held the world shot-put record not for decades, not for years, months, or even hours. Three minutes after he set the world record in 1964, his teammate Dallas Long broke it. Randy didn't even have time to get his sweats back on.

"Oh well, what the heck," Dick Fosbury might say. "The important thing is to do your thing your way. Don't try to be a carbon copy of somebody else." Dick—Fearless Fosbury to his friends—invented the craziest gyration that ever passed for a high jump. It was a circus flip-flop more than an athletic move, and even he couldn't explain how he did it. He had two bad feet and a rag-doll physique; but when he cleared the bar at seven feet 4¼ inches, nobody was laughing any more. And four years later at the Olympics in Munich, Germany, there were Fosbury floppers from all over the world.

Bob Beaman might point out to us that we ought not to set our sights too low. Who knows what was going through his mind as he sprinted the lane on to the long-jump pit in Mexico City in 1968. Probably he was just trying to beat the competition and maybe even set a record. What he did instead was practically go into orbit. When the disbelieving judges stretched out their tapes, Bob Beaman had sailed 29 feet 2½ inches—almost 2 feet beyond what any other man had ever jumped in recorded history. I don't think there has ever been such a quantum leap in any athletic endeavor. (Jon C. Halter, "The Record Breakers," *Boys' Life*, July 1980, pp. 37-48.)

Perhaps that is the best lesson of the Olympics to us. These athletes give us a glimpse of the incredible achievements a person can attain with single-minded dedication and purpose. *Citius, altius, fortius*—faster, higher, stronger; that is the Olympic motto. How fast, how high, how strong? What are the limits of the human body? What is the potential of a person? Frankly, we don't know.

Olympic records are standing testimonials to this principle. A physical goal seems impossible; then some super athlete achieves it. Then others begin to work on it with new confidence, knowing that it is possible. They equal the record. Then someone sets a new goal and shoots for it. It happens over and over and over again.

I asked a track coach who has trained a number of successful Olympians what are the limits of the human body. He said, "There must be some, and we used to know what they were—the four-minute mile, the eighteen-foot pole vault, the seven-foot high jump—all of these used to be impossible. But," he said, "we no longer talk about the impossible. We have been surprised too many times. We don't know what the potential of the human body is."

If the human body is thus far unmeasurable in its potential, what shall we say of the human mind and spirit? These are realms of achievement we have barely begun to explore and develop. Can you imagine what we as individuals and as a human race could achieve if we applied the same single-minded devotion in these areas that our athletes commit to in winning their medals? Every problem the world faces could be solved if we developed the same kind of prowess in honor, integrity, empathy, and morality that we have in athletics.

Furthermore, I believe that every person in the world could be a champion in this league. Each of us is gifted with unique abilities, talents, and skills that the world needs. When we determine to develop these talents—when we dedicate ourselves to using our best abilities to help others—we enter into the championship circle.

This is a far more important race than even the Olympics. It is a race in which there need be no losers. It is the race of life, the race the apostle Paul spoke of when he said, "They which run in a race run all, but one receiveth the prize. . . . Now they do it to obtain a corruptible crown; but we an incorruptible." (1 Corinthians 9:24-25.)

May we run our race of life like Olympic champions and obtain that incorruptible crown.

42

Victory at Sea,
Victory in Life

Over four decades ago a train shuttled across America from Washington, D.C., to the West Coast. Inside, disguised in civilian clothes, was a man deep in thought. He was about to take command over a great navy that had just suffered the worst defeat in American naval history—the carnage at Pearl Harbor. The "day of infamy," as President Franklin D. Roosevelt described it, had left twisted hulks of men and ships where the once proud Pacific fleet of the United States had sailed.

Americans were anguished, apprehensive, and angry at this failure of our navy to be prepared. How could he begin to restore the confidence of those who must have confidence if they were to eventually win? How could he begin to rebuild both ships and people into a fighting force? These were mammoth obligations and burdens, and upon the outcome of his acts might rest the fate of the nation.

The man's thoughts drifted back to his grandfather, who had become his counselor after young Chester's father died. "Life will give you challenges," the elderly man had said, "so you must be ready, must do your very best."

And right now Admiral Chester Nimitz would need his very best.

Later, as his plane swooped over Pearl Harbor, it was obvious that the damage was all that he had feared. As he entered his office as Commander-in-Chief, the uneasy looks on the faces of his staff members told him there was reconstruction work to be done here as well. They looked as though they wanted to be anywhere else in the world right now.

Admiral Nimitz thought of the times he had wanted to be elsewhere. He didn't want to be in the navy at all in the beginning. He wanted to be an army officer from West Point, but there were no openings, and so he went to the Naval Academy at Annapolis. Later on he wanted to command one of the big, beautiful battleships that were the pride of the fleet. Instead he was given one of those new-fangled tin cans that were designed to sink as well as float, those contraptions from the imagination of Rube Goldberg and the science fiction of Jules Verne—submarines.

He could have wasted time and energy bewailing his ill fortune, but instead Chester Nimitz learned what makes a submarine go, how a diesel engine works. He became one of the finest commanders in the Atlantic submarine fleet. This knowledge and the way he got it would now serve him well in the technical and strategic decisions he would have to make as commander in the Pacific.

The people on his staff were seeing themselves as failures, discouraged, despondent. He thought of the second ship he ever commanded way back before the first world war—a small and ancient destroyer named the *Decatur*. He remembered that in the poorly charted waters around the Philippines he had one night run his ship aground. He had to answer to a court-martial for that, and he thought it would cost him his command and earn him a desk for the rest of his career. But it didn't. He came back.

These people needed to know that they, too, could come back from defeat. So, in terms of the staff, Chester Nimitz did something unusual in that crisis. He did nothing. He did not demote anyone. He singled out no scapegoats. He did not try to shake things up and stir up fear. Instead, he let his staff know that theirs was a crisis—a problem and perhaps a mistake that could have happened to anyone— but that he still had confidence in them, and he was willing to put his career and even the fate of the country largely in their administrative hands. With this kind of total commitment and support, do you think those people reacted well and gave their absolute best to Chester Nimitz? History and his own writings record that they did.

But there was another very important segment of society that needed to be reassured. This was the American press and public. Chester Nimitz realized that, at this time of stress, nervousness, and near panic, someone needed to stand and be a symbol of calmness and self-control. He took this role upon himself. He had a horseshoe pit built near his home, and he often held press conferences there so that the reporters could feel the confidence he exuded in that setting. It worked well. The press carried the word to the people and helped them get over their anxieties and get to work in the enormous job of winning the war.

It was, as a matter of fact, on this backyard horseshoe pit that Admiral Nimitz spent part of one of the most important conflicts in naval history—the battle of Leyte Gulf. The struggling American navy trying to hold itself together and buy time to rebuild was nevertheless faced with a showdown against the mighty Japanese fleet, largely undamaged as yet in the war. The odds were not good for the Americans. Those who knew the situation were nervous.

It was at this point that Admiral Nimitz said to his staff, "I will be at home playing horseshoes. If there are any dispatches, you can reach me there." He had prepared as

well as he knew how. He had put good people in command-
ing posts and given them the confidence and authority to do
what needed to be done. He had tried to provide leadership
all up and down the line. He had listened to the best counsel
he could receive from commanders and common sailors
alike.

Now the outcome of the battle depended on hands
other than his, and he knew that. The best thing he could do
was try to keep calm and help others to keep calm. So,
though he was on pins and needles, he went back to throw a
few horseshoes. Years ago his grandfather had said, "After
you have done all you can, then don't worry about the outcome." He tried not to. We don't have a record of his horseshoe score, but I suspect it was not very good.

But the score of the American navy that day was his-
toric. They won the battle, saved the fleet, started America
on the course toward victory in the Pacific, and, just inci-
dentally, made a hero of Admiral Chester Nimitz and vin-
dicated his theories and style of leadership.

Yes, more battles are won by men than by machines—
men up and down the line with courage and resourcefulness
and character such as Chester Nimitz personified. And we
are eternally indebted to the millions of men and women
who saved our homeland and our freedom when they were
so gravely threatened.

But there is another side of the American fighting man
that again is typified by Chester Nimitz. In his hometown of
Fredericksburg, Texas—so far from tall ships and deep
water—is an unusually shaped hotel. Designed to look like a
big steamboat, it was built by his grandfather and has been
restored as a museum to the war in the Pacific. In the back is
a beautiful Japanese garden. At first you would assume it is a
memorial to the man who defeated the Japanese navy. But if
you thought such, you would be wrong on two counts. First
of all, it is dedicated not to Admiral Nimitz, but to the men

who fought under him. This is by the admiral's own request. And second, it was not built to honor the man who defeated Japan; rather, it was built to honor the man who realized that peace could never come through conquest, but only through mutual respect of one another as human beings.

And so, this victorious admiral chose this golden moment to respect his adversaries. He returned the ceremonial Samurai swords. He helped the Japanese rebuild for peace. He showed them respect. And they did not forget his gestures on their behalf. The Japanese garden behind the sturdy Steamboat Hotel was not built by his own government but came from voluntary contributions from the Japanese people themselves. It is not often that the vanquished voluntarily honor the victors.

And so, when I think of the terrible conflict that was World War II, I am inspired by men of character like Chester Nimitz, good men who would fight if necessary to preserve their homeland but who were ever quick to return to peace. May we honor their memory and rededicate our lives to the defense of our liberties here and to the extension of love and respect to every people, so that a dignified and lasting peace may cover the seas and the land.

43

The Father of Our Country

Recently a group of high school students were questioned about American history. They were only vaguely aware that Americans have ever had to fight for their freedom. They were blissfully naive of what it has taken to bring America to her present place.

We cannot be too critical of these young people, because we all suffer somewhat from the same historical astigmatism. We subconsciously assume that America just naturally grew into its present form of freedom and prosperity. But history tells us another story. The American revolution is unique in the annals of war and government. A number of fortunate circumstances brought this about, but one of the most important reasons the American revolution succeeded so spectacularly was George Washington.

Revolutions are not beneficial by nature. It just isn't built into the system. The revolutionary leader is usually a hard-driving and power-hungry personality ready to smash whatever stands in his way. But James Thomas Flexner wrote of Washington, "In all history few men who possessed unassailable power have used that power so gently and self-effacingly for what their best instincts told them was the welfare of their neighbors and all mankind." (*Washington, the Indispensable Man,* New York: New American Library, 1974, p. 14.)

The revolutionary general is usually a man of action not given to philosophical contemplation of the long-term patterns he is setting. Washington, on the other hand, was wise enough to see that others would follow the trail he marked out. He wrote, "I walk on untrodden ground. There is scarcely any part of my conduct which may not hereafter be drawn into precedent." Hugh Sidey commented on this: "That is at once beautiful and profound. It is no wonder he succeeded, entering office with such a code of conduct." (*Time,* February 21, 1983, p. 24.)

Yes, it requires one set of skills to be able to take power and almost an entirely different set of skills to use power once it is obtained. Rarely are these skills combined in the same person.

The revolutionary leader who achieves his objective is constantly on guard lest he lose the precious power he has struggled so hard and so dangerously to achieve. He inherits a situation in great flux and unsettled conditions. To protect himself, he usually institutes a very strict regulation of the country to quell any counterrevolts that might erupt before he gets his government firmly entrenched. These "temporary" measures almost always become permanent. The revolutionary is loath to give back power.

And so the history of revolutions in most nations has generally followed the same pattern. Dissidents overthrow a corrupt regime and then assume power. They clamp down on the people and merely replace one form of oppression with another. The list of world revolutions is one long tale of tragedy, bloodshed, and oppression.

But there is at least one inspiring exception amid the wreckage of abused and misused power the world has endured, one case in which a group of men were not society's outcasts and have-nots. They were men of means, successful leaders in their land. Their dream was not power, but freedom and the rights of all men.

Their leader by common consent was George Washington. Why? He was not as eloquent as Thomas Jefferson, not as intellectual as Alexander Hamilton, not as well-traveled and cultured as Benjamin Franklin. He was not a backslapping, persuasive politician nor a profound political philosopher. He won the war, but historians have never considered him a brilliant military strategist. The battle of Trenton, New Jersey, was one of the most important victories America ever won. It helped turn the tide of the war and persuaded the French to come to our aid. But technically the battle was a disaster.

As we all know from the famous picture, Washington crossed the Delaware River that winter night, but his was the only column to make it across. Two other columns failed. Once across, the Americans found their powder so wet that most of their guns were useless. Their position was hopeless, and Washington's commanders tried in vain to convince their general to retreat back across the river. The story has it that Washington stood on an old beehive in a muddy New Jersey field and single-handedly inspired his ragged forces to go on. America's freedom and her future rested that night on the stout heart of one man. May we ever be grateful that man was George Washington.

Courage and perseverance can also be characteristic of a fanatic or a power-mad megalomaniac. Washington was neither of these. Some of the sharpest condemnations he ever wrote were to well-meaning but misguided friends who wanted to make him a king or dictator. He wrote, "No occurrence in the course of the war has given me more painful sensations than your information of there being such ideas existing in the army." A dictatorship would bring "the greatest mischiefs that can befall my country," he added. (Flexner, p. 173.)

After achieving victory, Washington assumed the office of president of the United States virtually by acclamation. He showed the same outstanding leadership, wisdom, and command of the situation as president that he had as general. He brought to this new office dignity, respect, and the honor that it deserved. But he also set the pattern for service and for a dedication to the will of the people that set him apart from virtually any other revolutionary general turned president. He enthusiastically helped hammer out a government that would divide his power, not concentrate it in the chief executive, and that would put the military under the direction of civilian authority.

After serving nobly, humbly, and so well, Washington established another tradition by resigning his office and going home to his beloved Mount Vernon as a private citizen. He wanted no lifetime-ruler tradition established in this land he had given so much of his life to make free.

These traditions and others far too numerous to mention we owe to George Washington.

It has been fashionable the past few years to belittle and denigrate our heroes. I see signs that perhaps this fad is passing. I hope so, not so much for the sake of men like Washington, but for our own sakes. We need the noble examples of the past to guide us into the future. I firmly believe that God raised up these great personalities to whom we are so deeply indebted. I give thanks for the heritage these heroes have left us and pray that we may honor their names with our deeds.

44

The Pioneer Spirit

A pioneer past has not been totally buried under glass and concrete skyscrapers in Salt Lake City, Utah. In an occasional park, a log cabin that let the winter wind between its chinks or a wagon that carried all of the belongings of a family headed west is a reminder. But most of all, the pioneer past still burns in the minds of adults who remember curling up on their grandparents' knees to hear stories about it. "My grandmother was born on the trek," you'll hear them say.

What is there about the pioneers and the westward thrust that can still fire the imagination? Spencer W. Kimball said it this way: "Pioneers exemplified great determination and sacrifice. They had the persistence of ocean tides, which led them on; the strength of virgin forests, which braced their minds; the quiet of prairie vastness, which stilled their souls; the majesty of mountains, [which] gave them inspiration. These indomitable spirits faced the unknown with eyes upward and footsteps forward. There are men in this world who are made of adobe with a thin veneer carrying a high polish; but these men of the pioneer companies were of granite through and through. They did not shrink at difficult situations. . . . They went forth to conquer, and conquer they must and would, and did." (*Teach-*

ings of Spencer W. Kimball, Salt Lake City: Bookcraft, 1982, p. 178.)

I think, too, we are stirred by pioneer stories because they portray sacrifice and community spirit, which is so often missing in these days of instant pleasures and transience.

"Historians have called the Mormon migration [from Nauvoo, Illinois to Salt Lake City, Utah] the best-organized movement of people in American history." (Leonard J. Arrington and Davis Bitton, *The Mormon Experience*, New York: Alfred A. Knopf, 1979, p. 101.) That doesn't mean it was an easy movement. To prepare for the journey west, thousands of members of The Church of Jesus Christ of Latter-day Saints had to sell their farms and homes at a loss to get the money for a wagon and supplies. Martha Haven was typical of that group. "We have sold our place for a trifle," she wrote. "All we got was a cow and two pairs of steers, worth sixty dollars in trade." (Ibid, p. 97.) That was hardly enough for the requirements to head west, which included "one good wagon, three yoke of oxen, two cows, two beef cattle, three sheep, one thousand pounds of flour, twenty pounds of sugar, one rifle and ammunition, a tent and tent poles, from ten to twenty pounds of seed, and some farming tools." (Ibid, p. 95.) Such an outfit was necessary to see a family of five through the journey. Since many of the Saints didn't have that much, they had to stop frequently for employment in small Iowa towns along the way.

The earliest pioneer groups left Nauvoo in winter and set up their first camp in Iowa to wait for spring. They lived in the most primitive conditions there, and nine babies were born in freezing, dusty wagons or behind tent flaps. By the next fall they had crossed Iowa and spent the winter in Winter Quarters, where two hundred people died—or one in thirty.

That didn't stop them. "The Mormons went without

the guides and professional outfitters employed by most westering emigrants. A poverty-stricken band of people, in many cases unable to outfit themselves properly, the Saints were not frontiersmen; they were artisans, farmers, businessmen, and clerks." (Ibid., p. 101.)

When they arrived at their destination, there was no promise of comfort either. They planted crops on July 24, their first day of arrival in the Salt Lake Valley; but animals quickly grazed the untended shoots, and the first harvest was an inadequate supply of marble-sized potatoes. "By spring, the hungry farmers were reduced to eating crows, wolf meat, tree bark, thistle tops, sego lily bulbs, and hawks. Priddy Meeks's dilemma was typical. 'I would dig until I grew weak and faint and sit down and eat a root, and then begin again. I continued this until the roots began to fail.'"

These privations and sacrifices, however, helped forge a community spirit which made them survive. "We divided a bag of flour at Richardson's point, another at Charidon, and some more at the east fork of Shoal Creek and have enough to divide again if called for," pioneer Patty Sessions recorded in her journal at the end of two months' travel. Concern for the hunger of others became a way of life. Along the trail, weary pioneers stopped to plant gardens whose harvest would fill someone who came later. Once in the Salt Lake Valley, they sent back relief and supply parties to aid others on the last and toughest part of the route, and even when money was scarce, they found coins for a fund to finance the poverty-stricken who could not otherwise afford the journey.

We are not pioneers who forge into new lands and conquer the desert and who have to test our mettle every day for mere survival. We are not tried for our beliefs in a crucible of endurance. Yet all of us who, in a contemporary society, can build on their example must in fact embrace some of their qualities to survive our own spiritual journeys in the here and now. Are we willing to sacrifice for what we believe? Do our principles and ideals stir deeply enough within us so that our behavior conforms? Do we feel enough community spirit to plant crops for others, crops that we will never harvest? Do we muster enough strength to move beyond self-absorption to leave a trail of service behind us?

We are not pioneers, but our times demand just as much heroism and sacrifice, just as much service to one another, if we are to live well and true. It may be even more challenging when our situations don't force these characteristics upon us to develop them. But, as Spencer W. Kimball said, "Let us not lose the 'Winter Quarters' habit of starting crops to be harvested by those who follow. Let us be pioneers (for our people yet to be born) by planting the wheat of our witness, that those who follow us may eat of the bread of belief in time of famine elsewhere in the world!"

45

To Be a Champion

Most of us have sat in the stands or in front of the television set and watched champion athletes perform. In some ways they seem to be a special breed of men and women. We admire their quickness, speed, flowing coordination, and almost a sixth sense of how to play the game or compete in the contest. Yes, there is something special about a champion. No doubt about that. They seem to play so well, so easily.

Suppose, then, you saw a baseball team take the field that looked something like this. Their catcher had been an alcoholic and drug addict until he pulled his life together and got back to playing baseball. Their first baseman was fine in the field but an absolute disaster at the plate lately. He had come away empty his last fifteen times at bat. As a matter of fact, the team might have to put in their designated hitter. He had just made the team by the skin of his teeth at the first of the season, and that sort of thing doesn't inspire much confidence from the coaches or the crowd. They had to get something going from the plate, however, because their pitcher came hobbling in on a badly bruised knee. He had been hit by a line drive a couple of days earlier and had to be carried off the field.

In the words of the old baseball poem "Casey at the

Bat," "the outlook wasn't brilliant for the Mudville nine that day."

Perhaps the only thing that might encourage this team would be the troubles of the opposing club. Their manager who came limping onto the field really should have been in a rest home. He had recently had open-heart surgery and, not long after, had had one leg amputated.

All in all, this match-up of two problem-plagued, injury-prone, struggling ball clubs might bring out more pity than enthusiasm in the spectators. Certainly this was not the smooth, flawless, unruffled, untroubled display we associate with champions. And yet, at the end of this series, one of them would be crowned the champion, and the other would be runner-up as the greatest baseball teams of 1982. For this was the World Series between Milwaukee and St. Louis.

The alcoholic who had challenged and won over the toughest competition he ever faced and had then gone on to be named the team's most valuable player was Darrel Porter of St. Louis. The strikeout-king first baseman who had gone 0 for 15 was Keith Hernandez. How easy it would have been for him to go 0 for 20 and go back home. Instead, he reached way down deep inside, and in the critical last three games, he got three hits in game five, two more in game six, and hit a two-run single in game seven to tie the score.

The designated hitter who could have approached the plate intimidated since he just barely made the team at the first of the season chose instead to make his World Series one for the record books. He led all hitters with a cool .500 batting average for the series. He went 9 for 17 with four doubles and one triple and tied the record for most hits for a designated hitter in the World Series, a record he jointly holds with Hal McRae and Reggie Jackson. His name was Dane Iorg.

And what about Joaquin Andojar? He was the pitcher who had to be carried from the field in the first game of the series. He certainly had cause to sit this one out, collect his paycheck, and call it a season. Instead, he hobbled out to the mound for the crucial seventh game and came away as the winning pitcher for the world champion St. Louis Cardinals. In the other dugout, the prime candidate for a wheelchair was the Milwaukee manager, Harvey Kuehn. Instead of caving in to his problems, he ignored his missing leg and the long red scar on his chest from heart surgery and inspired his team to take the league championship, the playoffs, and almost the World Series.

Yes, there is something special about a champion. But it's not what most people think it is. Oh, certainly those who excel in sports and every other human endeavor have talent, but talent is not what separates the winners from the also-rans. Champions are not champions because they never fall down or strike out or stumble, but because they have the will to get back up every time they fall, and to try again.

Perhaps the greatest player ever in baseball was the immortal Babe Ruth. Until Hank Aaron bested his record, the Bambino was the greatest home-run hitter of them all, the greatest slugger in the game. But not everybody knows that Babe Ruth was also one of the great strikeout kings in baseball. In more than eight thousand times at bat, he walked away empty-handed hundreds of times. But did that intimidate him when he stepped to the plate? Did he hesitate and wonder? Not the Babe. He swung away with reckless abandon. Sometimes he would swing so hard that he would spin around and fall down at the plate, but he was willing to risk a few hoots from the fans to go for that centerfield wall. And inevitably he would come back and plant another one in the stands.

Champions don't quit when they're down. They keep coming back. It has been said that the amateur can perform as well as the professional, but he can't do it as consistently. A few months ago I noticed this statistic: The great golfer Jack Nicklaus earned $248,000 in 1982. Another golfer on the circuit earned about $48,000 that year, about one-fifth of Nicklaus's winnings. What was the difference in their golf scores over the season? Less than one stroke per eighteen holes. Perhaps there had been days when the other golfer wasn't feeling too well, his swing wasn't working, or his putts wouldn't drop, so he played good golf but not great golf. Nicklaus, on the other hand, had the dedication and concentration of a champion. Nothing could stop him from playing consistently fine golf.

The more I see of the real champions and succeeders in this world, the more I become convinced that natural aptitude and talent are not the secrets to their success. Rather it is the ability to overcome obstacles, including the obstacles we place in our own paths, that makes the difference between success and failure.

A prophet of the Lord centuries ago said there must needs be opposition in all things. (2 Nephi 2:11.) It is the way in which we face that opposition that determines whether or not we succeed. May the Lord help us to find the areas in which we can make our best contributions to the world and our fellowmen. Then may we go forth undeterred by opposition and problems and perform like champions.

46

The Quiet Hero

So much of history and headlines is filled with war, hatred, greed, corruption, crime, and violence that it can make you wonder how humanity even holds itself together. And then you read the story of Raymond Kolbe, and you know. The human race is held together and lifted slowly higher by the lives of the Raymond Kolbes among us. He was a hero in World War II, a quiet, small man with glasses, and with one lung filled with tuberculosis that he knew would never go away. His deeds are not etched on a heroic-sized marble monument. They are written in a rainbow arching from the hell of Auschwitz to the radioactive ruins of Nagasaki. His life is a halo over humanity connecting heaven and earth.

Kolbe won no great battles, liberated no nations. But at the Auschwitz prison camp he volunteered to starve to death in place of a husband and father who had been sentenced to that fate. And when his shriveled and emaciated frame was too tough to die after fourteen days without food or water, he quietly raised his bare arm with his prisoner's number 16670 indelibly tattooed on it and allowed the Nazi murderers to inject carbolic acid into his veins. The poison took his life, but it left his memory as one of the proud moments of human history. His body was incinerated in a crematorium he had been forced to help build with back-breaking labor.

Raymond Maximillian Kolbe was a Franciscan friar and was canonized as a saint not long ago by the Catholic church. His life would have been just one more nightmare in the sordid side of human history were it not for the man himself. He was a brilliant editor with degrees in philosophy and theology. He was an organizer and an indefatigable pioneer. He founded a successful newspaper and, on the outskirts of Warsaw, Poland, the largest Franciscan monastery in the world. It was a small city with a school, a hospital, a radio station, a printing plant, and even a fire station. On a hillside at Nagasaki, Japan, Father Kolbe constructed another center for Christian service. Interestingly, this was the only structure in the city still standing amid the radioactive ashes from the atom bomb.

Yes, Raymond Maximillian Kolbe was a builder of people and places, and as such he was a marked man when the Nazi destroyers moved in. They found him hiding two thousand Jews. They arrested him and turned his little city into a concentration camp. But death threats could not intimidate Father Kolbe, and captivity could not contain his spirit. His own father had chosen liberty over life and was hanged by the Russians as a freedom fighter.

Before Raymond Kolbe was thirty, doctors told him tuberculosis had destroyed one lung and would shortly eat through his other lung and end his life. Yet for all his bravery in facing death, perhaps even more inspirational was the way he stood up to the challenges of life and emerged triumphant. Coughing blood, wheezing behind his heavy-laden wheelbarrow, kicked in the stomach by his sadistic guards, scourged and starved, he refused to return hatred for hatred. He always answered his tormentors with a smile and a prayer. They could not beat the light of love out of him.

200

THE QUIET HERO

At Auschwitz, Bruno Borgoweic was the janitor and undertaker in the dreaded death cell block thirteen where Father Kolbe was sent to starve. Borgoweic said that every time he approached the cell to see who was still alive, he heard singing and prayers inside, and then the nearby bunkers joined in. Father Kolbe turned his underground dungeon into a heavenly chapel of hope. He learned well one of the most important lessons this life has to teach us if we will learn. He knew that ultimately we can direct our own destiny. We can create the world inside ourselves no matter how difficult our outward circumstances. The kingdom of God is within us, as Jesus said.

Father Kolbe learned and practiced another of the Lord's precepts. Jesus said, "Greater love hath no man than this, that a man lay down his life for his friends." (John 15:13.) Father Kolbe was willing to lay down his life not only for his friends, but for an unknown stranger whom he heard cry out in anguish when his name was read by the executioner. No, let me restate that. The man was not a stranger, for Raymond Kolbe knew no strangers. To him, every person he met under any circumstances was treated as a friend. He has been gone now more than forty years. But a life as nobly spent as his lives on as long as men love true nobility.

Emily Dickinson wrote, "Unable are the Loved to die, for Love is Immortality."

Certainly in a modest little home in Poland today there is a husband and father who will never forget how his life was handed to him as a willing sacrifice of Father Kolbe. In the minds and memories of those few who survived the savagery of Auschwitz and other prison camps, the little priest will live forever. And in the hearts of those who hear his story told and retold, this saintly man is a monument, a symbol of life lived at its very best. He makes us proud to belong to the human race and gives us hope that the finer spiritual side of our beings will eventually gently conquer the animal in us just as he conquered over his captors by the power of love and forgiveness.

May we strive to make this a better world so that lives like Raymond Maximillian Kolbe may not be wasted.

47

To Make a Man

John Huneke, a young man in his teens, lay in his hospital bed thinking deeply. He had a problem on his mind. If you didn't know John, you would guess that the problem was the bone cancer eating away his leg. Yes, that was serious, but John wasn't thinking about that. He was planning how he could finish up the work on his Eagle Scout badge and do the service project required of every aspiring Eagle.

The doctors had told him he couldn't get out of bed, so the usual civic projects weren't feasible. But then he thought of it. His nurses had told him the hospital was short of blood donors. John decided that his Eagle project would be to get a hundred donors to give blood to the hospital. The idea was sound, but the goal was completely out of perspective, John was told. He might get a couple of dozen donors with a lot of luck, but never a hundred.

Impossible was a word John was never very comfortable with, so he kept his goal at a hundred and set out to write letters and make phone calls to his friends in school, in scouting, and wherever he could find them. Several weeks later the hospital blood bank was indeed richer by one hundred pints, and John Huneke was carried on a stretcher to a scout court of honor convened in the hospital auditorium. Lying on his stretcher, he received from his mother that Eagle Scout badge he had so nobly earned.

For a moment the ceremony was stopped for a special announcement from the hospital. They had just processed their two hundredth blood donor courtesy of John Huneke's efforts. The hundred and fifty people in the audience stood and cheered this courageous young man.

Two weeks later Eagle Scout John Huneke was dead of bone cancer. He had done more good and developed more strength of character in his few short years than many of us will do in a lengthy lifetime. People will be healed and some may be saved from death because of the blood he collected. Untold thousands, perhaps millions will be moved to be better people because of his example. No eagle ever soared more loftily than John Huneke did from his hospital bed. (*Reader's Digest*, May 1982.)

Is scouting relevant today? You tell me. Are men like John Huneke needed in our world? Are love of God and dedicated service to country and to our fellow human beings relevant today? Then so is scouting, for that is what scouting is all about.

Scouting is much more than hiking in the hills and helping little old ladies across the street. Scouting's mission is to make men. And whenever it can help produce heroes of the stature of John Huneke, we can rest our case on the relevance of scouting.

Of course, times have changed since Lord Baden-Powell gathered his charges about him at Seal Island off the coast of England. He fired their spirits with true stories of his real scouting days as a British officer in the Boer war in Africa. But Lord Baden-Powell was not just regaling them with old war stories or picnics in the woods. Behind it all he had a very serious mission: to help these boys become men of integrity and character.

Today's boys still love to be in the woods and the mountains. It is the nature of boys. But they are also involved with computers, environmental affairs, business, education, and the thousand and one other activities going on in today's fascinating and fast-paced world. And because they are involved in today's world, so is scouting.

A modern scout is as likely to be working on a merit badge in computer science as in camping, in solar engineering as in swimming. He is learning to survive in society as well as the wilderness. He is learning to deal with today's changing world, but equally important, he is learning there are some things that do not change. A man's honor is still his most treasured possession. Enlightened patriotism and love of country are never outdated. The principles embodied in the scout laws are never repealed.

Julian Dyke, assistant to the chief scout executive of Boy Scouts of America, put it this way: "People ask me, . . . 'Is Scouting still relevant today?' I answer by saying, 'Well, if belief in God, if being of service to others, if becoming the very best person you can become, is being relevant, then the Boy Scouts of America is relevant, because that's what Scouting is all about.' That's what Scouting has always been, and Scouting's traditional value system remains the same today. Scouting's techniques and methods for marketing the resource program to the community-based organizations across America change, but the basic value system remains the same. I suggest that Scouting is what America at its best is all about. America needs Scouting today more than it ever has!" (Speech delivered at Gallaudet College in Washington, D.C., June 29, 1982.)

Scouting is still based on activity because boys love to be active. But mere activity in life is not enough. A few miles from San Jose, California, stands the famous Winchester Mystery House. It is a monument of sorts to the aimless construction that occupied most of the adult life of a wealthy widow who lived there, a sprawling 250-room monstrosity that covers six acres of real estate. There are doors that open on to blank walls, stairways leading nowhere, and windows looking out to nothing. The legend is that Mrs. Winchester believed her life would be prolonged as long as she kept the carpenters busy building on her house. Whatever her reasons, she left a graphic example of what a life of unplanned activity can create. At best it is a curiosity, and certainly the materials and means could have served a more significant purpose had they been guided by a plan.

Our lives are like that. Merely working is not enough. We must build from a plan. Scouting provides that plan for millions of young men throughout the world. It is an excellent plan, a plan of dedication, faith, and high ideals. It is the upward climb of the scouting trail. Real success in life is never an accident. It is the result of dedicated service to principles of honesty, reverence, service, and all that scouting has stood for and still stands for.

The reason the scouting trail is such a good plan is because it follows an even greater plan, a code of life given by the greatest builder of men and women who ever lived, the Lord Jesus Christ. He gave us the perfect example of living our lives in the service of others.

48

A Community of Friends

In August 1982, a young twenty-two-year-old man, David McNeice Jr., stood waiting for a Boston subway train to arrive when another man, screaming, abusive, and very drunk, wandered into the station, walked to the edge of the platform, and fell onto the tracks. Instantly, McNeice, responsible and married just three weeks, jumped to the track to help. At that second the train came out of the tunnel. McNeice frantically waved his arms but it was too late. He died beneath the wheels, and in one of those ironic twists of life, the drunken man survived the experience uninjured.

At first this might seem to be the story of a senseless death, a man who had everything to live for giving his life for nothing. But in this day of indifference to our fellow beings, McNeice's final gesture reverberates with eloquence, for it says what we so often forget: that every human being, no matter how apparently worthless or derelict, no matter how distant or different from ourselves, is our brother. Because we are human, we share in a community of tears and hopes and pains and dreams with more in common than we ever begin to understand.

The speed with which David McNeice responded to the drunken man's plight tells us that it was probably instinctive, a recognition that had probably grown through his entire lifetime that he was somehow his brother's keeper. And if it is not a recognition that we have nurtured, it is probably time to do something about it. Nothing is more important than to learn to live wisely and responsibly together.

Our fellow human beings with whom we rub shoulders and fight for parking spots and theater tickets are not strangers, even if we do not know them. We are a community, highly dependent on each other.

Those who first came to this country on the *Mayflower* saw themselves as a community, realizing it anew every time they were tossed by the waves of the ocean, every time they divided their meager food. They were coming to a land where none of them could make it alone. There were no soloists, eager to fight off the beasts and stave off hunger without help. They even signed a compact to make their dependence on each other official, claiming that they would work "for the glory of God, the advancement of the Christian faith, and the general good of the Colony."

One hundred and fifty years later, Benjamin Franklin affirmed the same idea to the signers of the Declaration of Independence. "We must all hang together," he said with a touch of dry humor, "or assuredly we shall all hang separately." And though Franklin undoubtedly meant his warning literally—the Founding Fathers could have hung had they failed—the idea applies in a more general sense today.

If we see our fellow beings as enemies or even anonymous strangers whose concerns do not affect us, our own lives will be that much diminished and our communities will fail. If our concerns extend no further than how to get our own lunch, then we will have missed the point of why we were put here together in the first place. T. S. Eliot said it this way: "Hell is oneself. Hell is [experienced] alone. There is nothing to escape from and nothing to escape to."

And we can be assured that heaven is quite the opposite—a community of friends where each does his part because he realizes that the greater good has something to do with him. Human bonds are to be cherished.

This sense of brotherhood, this sense of larger community, is probably undermined today by two forces.

The first undermining force is indifference to one another. We watch the drunk fall on the subway tracks and ask, "So what?" We say the same thing when we see masses of human beings suffering on the evening news. Perhaps the sheer numbers of people with whom most of us live spawn that attitude. There were only a few more than a hundred pilgrims on the *Mayflower*, each one precious for what he brought the community, each one missed when he was gone. Today we live in cities and traffic jams and high-rise apartments, and we excuse ourselves for viewing humanity as only so many hunks of flesh and bone because, after all, there are so many.

But has the principle changed? We are still dependent on each other, and each is still our brother. Our task is still the same: to work together for the good of us all, recognizing the kinship we have with every soul who walks this planet. We are still called to feed the hungry, visit the sick, and mourn with those who mourn—not just shut ourselves up in our houses and watch TV. Who will help those who need help if we don't do it?

The second force that undermines our community sense is the attitude that suggests, "What I do doesn't matter anyway." Too many of us are missing the conviction that our community will only be as good as we are—or as bad as we are. An old Arabic legend tells of a rider finding a spindly sparrow lying on its back in the road. He dismounted and asked the sparrow why his feet were in the air.

Replied the sparrow, "I heard the heavens were going to fall today."

"And I suppose you think your puny bird legs can hold up the whole universe?" scoffed the horseman.

"Perhaps not," said the sparrow with conviction, "but one does what one can."

Being part of a network of humanity means that we are called upon to do whatever we can. We must always be asking ourselves, "Have I done my part? Have I done what I am capable of doing?"

Think about how those who succumb to their weaknesses afflict us all. There are no victimless crimes. Those who turn to drugs or crime, those who are self-seeking, those who are callous to suffering—all of these pull down the entire community. Standards degrade, ideals are tarnished, and communities evolve according to the attitudes of their members. But those who find their strengths can lift us, buoy us, and point us heavenward. We are all richer for a David McNeice who would jump on the tracks for a stranger.

The message of this life is to care, finally understanding that the greatest lesson of life is perhaps the most obvious one. We weren't put here alone but in a community, because we have more to learn in friendship than in self-centeredness, more to gain in giving than seeking, and ironically because our self-interest is best served in serving others.

Index

Wannamaker, John, 80
Washington, George, 186-89
Whitman, Walt, 36, 125
Wilson, Earl, 94
Winchester Mystery House, 204-5
Winning, meaning of, 173-76. *See also*
    Champions; Success
Wolfe, Tom, 60
Work, full day's, 81-82
World, how we see, 55-58, 72-75

World Series, 194-96
World War II, U.S. Navy in, 181-85
Wright, Orville, 19
Wright, Wilbur, 19

Yankelovich, Daniel, 60

Zerof, Herbert G., 113-14
Zorens, Ted, 86-87